SUB-AQUA ILLUSTRATED DICTIONARY

SUB-AQUA
Illustrated Dictionary

Leo Zanelli and George Skuse

KAYE & WARD · LONDON
OXFORD UNIVERSITY PRESS
NEW YORK

First published in Great Britain by
Kaye & Ward Ltd
21 New Street, London EC2M 4NT
1976

First published in the USA by
Oxford University Press Inc.
200 Madison Avenue,
New York, N.Y. 10016, USA
1976

ISBN 0 7182 1136 7 (Great Britain)
ISBN 0-19-519894-8 (USA)
Library of Congress Catalog Card No. 76-16693

Filmset by Computer Photoset, Birmingham, England
Printed in Great Britain by Cox & Wyman Ltd
London, Fakenham and Reading

FOREWORD

This book has been designed to fill a gap in available sub-aqua literature. We must confess, though, that writing it produced more difficulties than were first envisaged; and we are painfully aware that it will probably both please and displease most readers.

Some of the difficulties were obvious – providing hundreds of facts and, at the same time, trying to ensure accuracy despite human and typographical errors, for example. Then there was the problem of deciding what to leave out. This is always a difficulty with dictionaries, but in the case of sub-aqua diving, which touches on boating, photography, biology and many other subjects, this becomes a very real problem. The greatest problem, however, was in trying to produce a text for people of differing standards. The non-diver, for instance, in looking up 'twin-hose regulator', will want to know exactly what that piece of equipment looks like. On the other hand, the diver will already know, but may be interested in some of the more technical, less obvious features such as 'balanced valves'. Illustrations therefore have to be provided in both cases. Either may please/displease, depending on the requirements and standard of the reader.

We hope that, in spite of all these factors, we have struck a reasonable balance. The non-diver will find most of the popular terms and equipment simply named, described and, where possible, illustrated. Likewise the diver – even an advanced one – should find much of value in this book, particularly when studying for examinations or qualifications, apart from using it for general reference.

This is, as far as we know, the first time a book of this nature has been produced, and we would certainly appreciate comments – favourable or otherwise.

Leo Zanelli
George Skuse

A

A.B.L.J. °Adjustable buoyancy life-jacket.

absolute pressure The 'true' or total pressure being exerted at any point. It *includes* atmospheric pressure. Thus the absolute pressure at sea level is 14·7 psi or one atmosphere, and at 33 ft or 10 m it is 29·4 psi or two atmospheres.

absolute zero The lowest temperature attainable ($-459°$F or $-273°$C). This figure is necessary for calculations involving gas pressures; °gas laws.

accessory Any piece of equipment that is not essential to underwater use, but which makes diving easier or safer, e.g. depth gauge, watch, knife.

acetylene Inflammable gas used in welding above water. It becomes unstable (explosive) at pressures above two atmospheres, and so should never be used under water.

A-clamp Device for clamping charging hoses, regulators or manifolds to air cylinder pillar valves; °ill. 1.

activated (Related to charcoal or alumina.) Treated in such a way that their powers of adsorption are considerably increased. Used as a filter medium in compressors to remove traces of oil, water and solid particles from the compressed air.

activated alumina Special form of aluminium oxide.

activated charcoal Carbon made from coconut husk, wood, bone, etc.

adjustable buoyancy lifejacket (A.B.L.J.) Lifejacket worn by diver which may be fully or partially inflated under water to compensate for negative buoyancy; or to enable the diver to surface in a hurry in an emergency. The inflation gas is air, by mouth inflation, or from a separate cylinder, or by 'direct feed' from the aqualung cylinder; °buoyancy compensator; °lifejacket.

adsorption Process of concentrating molecules upon the surface of a solid.

aerodon talgia Pain in a tooth caused by compressed air expanding. Also caused by compression of a gas (air) space beneath a filling, causing that filling to move.

1. A-clamp

1

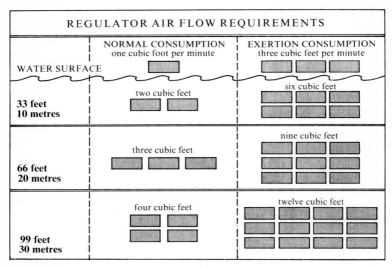

REGULATOR AIR FLOW REQUIREMENTS

2. Showing the quantity of air required for a diver to maintain ambient pressure (*U.S. Divers*)

'A' flag Flag in the International Code of Signals which indicates: 'I have a diver down, keep well clear and at slow speed'. Commonly called flag Alpha, it has been adopted by most of the world's diving organisations, including the World Underwater Federation, as the diving flag; °ill. 21.

aft Towards the stern; in the rear part of a boat.

after drop When a person suffering °hypothermia is placed in a warm environment, the core temperature may actually drop before rising again. This may be due to the return of extremely cold blood from the limbs to the core with increasing circulation. The drop can be as much as 2°C (approx. 4°F) and can be lethal.

ahead Forward, or ahead of a boat.

air composition Approximate: nitrogen 78%, oxygen 21%, inert gases 1%, carbon dioxide 0·03%, variable amounts of water vapour. Exact (dry air):

	% by volume	% by weight
Nitrogen	78·09	75·54
Oxygen	20·93	23·14
Argon	0·93	1·27
Carbon dioxide	0·03	0·05
Neon Helium Krypton Hydrogen Xenon Ozone	0·02	0·00

air consumption There are many standards of air consumption. As a very rough guide, it can be assumed that a person walking steadily consumes 1 cu. ft or 25 litres of air per minute. (This conversion is approximate.) But air consumption varies widely with each individual; °oxygen consumption.

air density Dry air at 0°C (32°F) and 760 mm mercury. 1·293 gm/l or 0·0807 lbs/ft³.

air embolism Air in the bloodstream. Blockage of one or more blood vessels by a bubble of air. Usually a result of °barotrauma.

air endurance This relates directly to air consumption and depends on (*a*) individual metabolism, fitness and degree of exertion; (*b*) air cylinder capacity; (*c*) depth; (*d*) degree of experience and emotional state; °ill. 2.

air filter °Filter, air.

air lift A device for raising small objects or silt, etc. from the bottom of a body of water. It forces a stream of air bubbles into the bottom of a hose or tube; bubbles float up the hose and cause it to function rather like a vacuum cleaner.

air purity Pure air is that which is found in nature uncontaminated by man or by processes of decay, etc. It is frequently difficult to set a suitable standard of purity and then to get air of that standard.

air purity standards There are many, all slightly different, e.g. United States Navy, Canadian Standards Association, British Standards Association (B.S. 4001), B.S.A.C., etc.

air reservoir A large static air cylinder used in conjunction with a compressor. It permits more rapid filling of air cylinders than the compressor alone can achieve; °decanting.

air testing A means of discovering whether a given sample of air is within a stated standard of purity. Accurate analysis is carried out by a gas chromatograph. Approximate analysis is carried out by drawing known quantities of air over chemical reagents and noting any colour change.

airway 1. The air passage of nose, mouth, pharynx, larynx and trachea by which air passes to the lungs. **2.** A tube introduced into the above to keep them open during unconsciousness.

air weight Air, at normal atmospheric pressure, has a specific weight. This may be taken as $1\frac{1}{4}$ gm/l or 0·08 lbs/cu. ft; °air density.

alcohol Ethyl alcohol (C_2H_5OH) is the active ingredient of alcholic drinks. It reduces tolerance to cold and increases the effects of nitrogen narcosis. Diving should not take place within four hours of consuming alcohol, or while 'hung over'.

algae The group of non-flowering plants called the seaweeds (there are freshwater varieties). The three most important groups are: chlorophyta – green algae; phaeophyta – brown algae; rhodophyta – red algae.

alloy A mixture of two or more metals. With such a mixture the properties of both metals might be improved.

alpha Phonetic for letter 'A'; °'A' flag.

alternobaric vertigo Vertigo, giddyness and/or loss of orientation or balance resulting from pressure changes in the ear; due to changes in depth and/or ear clearing.

altitude Height above sea level. Whether on land or in an aircraft, this can affect °decompression.

alumina Aluminium oxide. Used as a dessicant in compressor filters, usually in the form of °activated alumina.

aluminium Metal element. Ductile, malleable and light in weight. Resistant to corrosion. A useful component of an °alloy.

alveolus 1. Terminal air-sac in the lungs where gaseous exchange takes place. **2.** Cavity or socket in jaw bone into which a tooth fits.

ambient Immediately surrounding. Generally used of temperature or pressure.

amphora Ancient earthenware vase. In ancient times used for the transport and storage of liquids, especially oil or wine.

anaesthetic A substance, in gas or liquid form, which causes a loss of feeling, insensibility or unconsciousness; °nitrogen narcosis; chloroform.

analgesic A remedy which relieves pain.

analysis °Air testing.

anchor In effect a weighted hook placed on or in the sea bed and attached to a boat via rope or chain. Horizontal pull is needed for efficient anchoring (°anchor warp). Holding power depends on bottom; °anchor size; °C.Q.R.; °Danforth; °fisherman anchor.

anchoring The practice of dropping and securing the °anchor to hold the vessel in a specific place.

anchor size Calculation for °fisherman anchor: up to 9 ft (3 m) boat – 4 lbs (1·8 kg). Add 1 lb (0·45 kg) per extra foot or 300 mm. Reduce weight by $\frac{1}{3}$ for °Danforth or °C.Q.R., but increase weight by $\frac{1}{3}$ for over-night mooring.

anchor warp Minimum length is 3 times the maximum depth at the site. The optimum length is 5 times the depth. Anchor should be attached to warp by a spliced eye.

ankle straps °Fixe-palmes; °ill. 3.

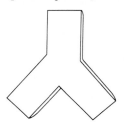

3. Ankle strap

anneal A heat treatment for metal or glass. Material is heated then cooled. It has the effect of hardening some metals, e.g. duralumin, and softening others, e.g. copper.

anode Positive electrode.

anoxia Total lack of oxygen; this is rare. Acute anoxia (instantaneous anoxia) occurs when cylinders have been filled with e.g. nitrogen only. Unconsciousness occurs within 30 seconds; °hypoxia.

anticyclone Meteorological state of high atmospheric pressure, usually denoting fine weather.

antihistamine A group of drugs which (among other things) helps control travel sickness. Not as effective as hyoscine, but better tolerated for long journeys. Can cause drowsiness, and add to the effects of hypnotic drugs and/or alcohol. Should not be taken before or during a dive.

anxiety Mental state which can increase exhaustion and the effects of cold. It often precedes panic.

aqualung The common British name for scuba; °scuba pack; °ill. 51, 52 and 53.

aqua-lung The name, registered in some countries, for the regulator/air cylinder combination devised by °Cousteau and °Gagnan. Marketed in France 1947, Britain 1950, Canada 1951 and U.S.A. 1952.

aquaplane A predominantly flat surface or board towed by a boat and controlled by a diver, so that he may cover a large area rapidly when searching.

arc (electric) Highly luminous, high temperature discharge. Used in underwater cutting and welding. Also the source of light in arc-lights; °oxy-arc.

Archimedes' Principle (Law) When a body is wholly or partially immersed in a fluid, e.g. water, it experiences an apparent up-thrust. This up-thrust is equal to the weight of fluid displaced.

Argentina Federation Argentina de Actividades Subacuaticas,Casilla de Coreo, Puerto Madryn, Provincia de Chubut, Argentina.

argon An inert gas occurring as 0·8% of atmospheric air. Used in filling electric lamps, and as a substitute for oxygen in the oxy-arc cutting torch.

artery A major blood vessel which carries blood away from the heart.

artificial respiration A means of oxygenating the blood of a person without the help of that person; °resuscitation.

ascent, assisted An ascent where both divers ascend sharing one aqualung.

ascent, buoyant Ascent where extra buoyancy has been gained by inflating a lifejacket or, to a lesser extent, by

dropping the weightbelt. It cannot be stopped unless relief valves are fitted to the lifejacket and frequently involves acceleration near the surface. Many navies use this method for submarine escape.

ascent, emergency Any ascent other than normal.

ascent, free Ascent without using the aqualung and without additional buoyancy.

ascent hazards 1. Hitting a surface obstruction. **2.** Barotrauma through breath-holding, ascending too fast or having a lung lesion. **3.** Decompression sickness. **4.** Exhaustion from surfacing when 'heavy' or negatively buoyant. **5.** Losing your buddy.

ascent, normal Fin gently to the surface at 15 m (18 m or 60 ft on some tables) per minute, keeping in contact with your buddy and glancing towards the surface for obstructions, e.g. boats. The hand is usually held above the head.

ascent rate °Ascent, normal.

asdic Anti Submarine Detection Investigation Committee; °sonar.

aseptic bone necrosis Non-infectious death of bone leading to arthritis and possible bone collapse. A long-term effect of living under pressure or possibly undetected decompression sickness; °decompression sickness.

asphyxia Suffocation; °inability to draw air into the lungs. The usual cause of death in drowning.

aspirin A drug (acetylsalycilic acid) used alone or with other ingredients to relieve pain (analgesic) or reduce temperature (anti-pyretic). It may increase body heat loss in a diver.

astern Behind a boat.

asthma Spasm of muscles within the lungs affecting respiration. Emotionally induced asthma is a disqualifying factor for divers. Advice should be sought from a diving doctor.

at(s) Abbreviation for the unit of pressure 'atmosphere(s)'.

ata Abbreviation of atmospheres absolute pressure.

atmosphere 1. The air surrounding the Earth. **2.** A unit of pressure equivalent to that exerted on the surface of the Earth by the atmosphere.

atmospheric pressure At zero°C (32°F) at sea level, equivalents: 14·7 psi; 1014 milibars (approx. one bar); $102 kN/m^2$; $1033·3 gm/cm^2$.

atrium An upper chamber of the heart which receives blood from the veins and passes it to the ventricle. The left atrium receives oxygenated blood, the right one de-oxygenated blood.

attendant The person above water who cares for a diver under water. He helps him get ready and enter the water, attends the safety line constantly and helps the diver leave the water.

aural Pertaining to the ear and/or hearing.

aural barotrauma Damage to the ear(s) due to pressure changes during descent or ascent; °ear clearing; °ears; °reversed ears.

auricle °Atrium.

Australia Australian Underwater Federation, 24 Victoria Street, New Lambton, N.S.W. 2305, Australia. Founded 1947.

Austria Tauchsportverband Osterreichs, Karoliengasse 25/6, A 1040 Wien, Austria. Founded 1967.

automatic reserve °R-reserve.

Avogadro's Hypothesis (Law) Equal volumes of gases at the same temperature and pressure contain the same number of molecules.

B

backing When the wind changes direction in an anti-clockwise manner.

back pack °Harness; °ill. 53.

bag lifting A bag designed to be inflated with air to lift objects. Particularly useful in salvage work. To allow for air expansion as the bag ascends, it must either be open at the bottom or be fitted with a pressure relief valve.

balanced valve A valve controlling the passage of high pressure air in such a way that the air pressure does not affect the force needed to operate the valve; °downstream; °upstream; °ill. 4.

balloon surfacing A diver in a dry suit, who over-inflates the suit surfacing rapidly, tends to come up spreadeagled with his suit swollen or ballooning.

bangstick An explosive device commonly carrying a 12-bore or smaller cartridge at the end. On contact with the victim (usually a shark) the

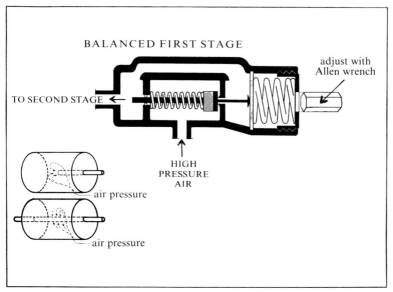

BALANCED FIRST STAGE

adjust with
Allen wrench

TO SECOND STAGE ←

HIGH
PRESSURE
AIR

air pressure

air pressure

4. Balanced first stage of a single hose *(U.S. Divers)*

cartridge detonates and the shock wave kills the shark.

bar A unit of pressure approximating that of one °atmosphere; 1,000 millibars; °atmospheric pressure; °millibar.

Bargellini, Alberto Veteran Italian diver of the Sorima Salvage Company of Genoa. In August 1930, he descended to a depth of 426 ft in an armoured diving suit designed by Neufeldt & Kuhnke of Germany – far deeper than any diver had ever been. He worked on the salvage of gold from the *Egypt*. While working on a wrecked U.S. munitions ship, *Florence H*, the wreck blew up, killing Bargellini and 13 others.

barometer Instrument for measuring °atmospheric pressure.

barometric Appertaining to pressure as measured by a °barometer.

barotrauma Physical damage to the body as a direct result of expanding or contracting air; °aural barotrauma; °burst ears; °ears; °embolism; °emphysema; °pneumothorax; °reversed ears; °squeeze.

Barton, Otis American geologist and engineer who designed °Beebe's °bathysphere. He and Beebe made the first test descent down to 800 ft in June 1930. Later, in 1934, the two of them reached 3,028 ft in the bathysphere.

basic equipment The minimum necessary for snorkelling or 'skin' diving, i.e. mask, fins and snorkel.

AS USED AT SEA

Beaufort International Number	Wind	Units of speed		Indications at sea
		Nautical miles per hours (knots)	Feet per second	
0	Calm	Less than 1	Less than 2	Sea mirror smooth.
1	Light air	1–3	2–5	Small wavelets like scales, no foam crests.
2	Light breeze	4–6	6–11	Waves short and more pronounced; crests begin to break; foam has glassy appearance – not yet white
3	Gentle breeze	7–10	12–18	
4	Moderate breeze	11–16	19–27	Waves are longer; many white horses
5	Fresh breeze	17–21	28–36	Waves now pronounced and long; white foam crests everywhere.
6	Strong breeze	22–27	37–46	Larger waves form; white foam crests more extensive.
7	Strong wind	28–33	47–56	Sea heaps up; wind starts to blow the foam in streaks.
8	Fresh gale	34–40	57–68	Height of waves increases visibly; also height of crests; much foam is blown in dense streaks.
9	Strong gale	41–47	69–80	
10	Whole gale	48–55	81–93	High waves with long overhanging crests; great foam patches.
11	Storm	56–65	94–110	Waves so high that ships within sight are hidden in the troughs; sea covered with streaky foam; air filled with spray.
12	Hurricane	Above 65	Above 110	

8

IND SCALE

Wind	Unit of Speed Statute m.p.h. recorded at 33 ft above ground level	Indications on land	Diving outlook
Calm	Less than 1	Smoke rises vertically.	**Excellent**
Light air	1–3	Direction shown by smoke but not by wind vanes.	**Excellent**
Light breeze	4–7	Wind felt on face; leaves rustle, ordinary vanes moved by wind.	**Very good**
Gentle breeze	8–12	Leaves and small twigs in constant motion; wind extends light flag.	**Good**
Moderate breeze	13–18	Raises dust and waste paper; small branches are moved.	**Care needed**
Fresh breeze	19–24	Small trees in leaf begin to sway; crested wavelets form on inland waters.	**Great care needed**
Strong breeze	25–31	Large branches in motion; whistling heard in telegraph wires; umbrellas used with difficulty.	
Moderate gale	32–38	Whole trees in motion; inconvenience felt when walking against wind.	
Fresh gale	39–46	Breaks twigs off trees; greatly impedes progress.	**NO DIVE**
Strong gale	47–54	Slight structural damage occurs (chimney pots and slates removed).	
Whole gale	55–63	Seldom experienced inland; trees uprooted; considerable structural damage occurs.	
Storm	64–75	Very rarely experienced; accompanied by widespread damage.	
Hurricane	Above 75		

basic training The minimum training given to enable a diver to use scuba under water – this only covers a swimming pool or hazard-free, still, shallow, open water.

Bass, Dr George F. Underwater archaeologist. Formal academic training in classical studies and classical archaeology. Doctorate, University of Pennsylvania. Directed underwater excavations at Cape Gelidonya and Yassi Ada; author of *Archaeology Under Water*.

bathymeter A simple depth-gauge depending on the effect of pressure (according to °Boyle's Law) on a bubble or air trapped in a capillary tube.

bathyscaphe Deep diving vehicle carrying its own buoyancy as a (virtually) incompressible liquid, e.g. petrol. Invented by Prof. Auguste Piccard. One version reached a depth of 35,800 ft (approx. 12,000 m) in 1960.

bathysphere A pressure-proof sphere lowered to great depths on a cable from a surface vessel. Designed by Otis Barton and shared by Dr William Beebe, it descended to 3,028 ft (approx. 1,000 m) in 1934.

beam The width of a boat.

beam sea A sea running at right-angles to the vessel's course, causing the vessel to roll.

bearing The angular directions of an object expressed with reference to a compass bearing or another object.

bearing, compass A bearing in terms of compass degrees from North. May be magnetic or true.

bearing, hand Bearing taken with a hand-held compass.

bearing, transit Bearings taken by lining up two objects – usually fixed items such as buildings – ashore.

beating the lung Breathing or attempting to breathe faster than the scuba unit can deliver air. This leads to panic, hypoxia, etc.; °breathlessness.

Beaufort wind scale A system for assessing conditions at sea; °ill. 5.

Beebe, Dr William Beebe was an academically trained American scientist, who was already famous before he went under water with a Dunn helmet in the 1920s. He later descended to 3,028 ft in the bathysphere with °Barton. Author of *Half Mile Down*.

Behnke, Dr A. R. A U.S. navy doctor, Behnke did valuable research work on helium mixtures and tables, in conjunction with Dr O. D. Yarbrough, starting in 1937.

belay To make a rope fast; to stop any activity.

Belgium Belgische Federatie voor Onderwateronderzoek en Sport, avenue Jules Colle 5, B 1410 Waterloo, Belgium. Founded in 1957.

bell, diving °Diving bell.

Belloni, A. Italian designer of a system of escape from submerged submarines. The system is described by him as the 'tube (or trunk) and tub method, on the Torricelli barometric principle'.

bend (knot) A knot joining one piece of rope to another; °hitch (knot).

bends A form of decompression sickness, so called because certain bent positions ease the pain.

berried Bearing eggs on the outer surface of the body, e.g. crabs.

bezel A rotating collar round a watch used to note elapsed time on a diving watch.

bilge The very bottom of a boat inboard. The lowest part other than the keel outboard.

billy, shark A short stick with or without a point or nail in the end used for fending off sharks. It is not intended to wound.

biology The study of life and living things.

blackout Unconsciousness; °shallow water blackout; °syncope.

blob buoy A small surface buoy towed on a line by a diver. Used to indicate his underwater position to anyone on the surface.

bleeding 1. Loss of blood from the body. **2.** The release of small quantities of air from a cylinder. **3.** The release of small quantities of fluid from a hydraulic system.

blood pressure Usually measured as the height of a column of mercury which the blood can support. Measured in the brachial artery, the systolic pressure is 120-140 mm mercury, and 70 mm mercury diastolic.

blowing up Another name for °balloon surfacing.

boat box A waterproof container of tools, spares, flares, first aid kit, etc., carried on a small diving boat.

B.O.D. Biochemical oxygen demand; a way of expressing the amount of oxygen needed to purify sewage or other contaminated water. A high B.O.D. indicates the death of large numbers of fish and other animals in the water.

bollard A post, aboard or ashore, used for fastening a line when mooring a boat.

bolt gun Gun using an explosive cart-ridge to fire a steel bolt into iron, steel or concrete.

bone necrosis °Aseptic bone necrosis.

boot 1. Rubber or plastic receptacle fitted to the base of an air cylinder to protect it and enable it to stand upright; °ill. 6. **2.** Shoe or foot-fitting part of a wet suit; sometimes called a bootee.

6. Boot for holding a cylinder or tank

Borelli, Alfonso An Italian who designed an independent diving dress in 1679. It included claw-like footwear, but the diver walked on the sea bed.

Borghese, Prince Valerio J. He commanded an Italian submarine in General Franco's service during the Spanish Civil War. Commander of the Italian underwater 'chariot' team during World War II. Author of *The Sea Devils*.

bottle Name for any size of cylinder containing compressed air; °tank.

bottom time The time elapsed from leaving the surface until starting the ascent. This is the time required for decompression calculations.

11

Bourdon tube A curved metal tube which tends to straighten when subjected to internal pressure. It is the pressure detector in most pressure gauges and many depth-gauges.

Boutan, Louis Underwater photography pioneer. Lecturer in the Faculty of Science of Paris, attached to the Arago Laboratory in Banyuls, France. In 1893, Boutan applied himself to the problem of photography under water. Working with a clumsy helmet suit, he first experimented with a completely flooded camera, using specially varnished plates. Dissatisfied, he developed a watertight camera and succeeded in taking some of the first underwater photographs. His book *La Photographie Sousmarine*, published in 1900, is almost certainly the first book on the subject.

bow The front end of a boat.

bower anchor The main anchor.

bowline One of the most useful knots, used for securing safety lines to divers; °ill. 7.

7. Bowline

Boyle, Robert An Englishman, Boyle was one of the first people to study the effects of decompression. His book, *New Experiments, physico-mechanical, touching the spring of air, and its effects*, was written in 1660; it explained the barometer and outlined °Boyle's Law.

Boyle's Law At a constant temperature, the absolute pressure of a gas is inversely proportional to its volume.

bradycardia Slowing of the heartbeat. It occurs when the face is immersed in water. Diving mammals display extreme bradycardia, e.g. the pulse in seals, normally about 80/minute, falls to 8/minute during a dive.

brass An alloy of copper and zinc; °restoration.

Brazil Confederacao Brasiliera de Deportes, Rue de Alfandega 70, Rio de Janeiro, Brazil. Founded in 1914 as a general sporting organization.

breath-holding Voluntary cessation of breathing. Only possible by great willpower in conscious persons. The time can be extended by °hyperventilation.

breathing The process of moving air in and out of the lungs.

breathing resistance Personal resistance stated to be 4 cm water/litre air/second. Add equipment resistance to total 7·5 cm water/litre air/second as desirable limit, but up to 12 cm water/litre air/second may be accepted occasionally. 12 cm water/litre air/second is reached at a pressure equivalent to 264 ft on air (9 ata) by man alone with no apparatus resistance. Ideally the expiratory resistance should not exceed 6 cm water/litre air/second, and should never exceed inspiratory breathing resistance.

breathlessness A diving hazard which can lead to panic. Stages: 1. Transitory – initial breathlessness during an 'oxygen debit' situation. CO_2 is soon eliminated and respiration becomes normal. 2. Slight carbon dioxide poisoning. 3. Severe carbon dioxide poisoning leading to unconsciousness. Causes: Emotional stress; physical exertion and fatigue; poor breathing technique; cold; hangover; poor physical fitness; °beating the lung; equipment faults.

British Standards Institution A non-profitmaking concern which sets standards of quality, etc. for materials, apparatus and equipment. Goods approved are marked with the 'Kite Mark'. British Standard numbers of interest to divers are: 3595 (life-saving jackets); 4001 Part I (care and maintenance of underwater breathing apparatus – compressed air, open circuit type), Part II (standard diving equipment); 1319 (colour of gas cylinders); 1780 (pressure gauges); and 4532 (snorkels and face masks).

broach to Boating term meaning to turn (involuntarily) broadside on to the waves. This can lead to swamping or capsizing.

bronze medallion Award of the Royal Life-Saving Society; °sub-aqua bronze medallion.

bronze, phosphor Bronze improved by the addition of up to 1% phosphorus.

Broussard, Henri Leading French underwater pioneer. The initiative for the first Underwater Archaeology Conference, held at Cannes in 1955, came from Broussard.

B.S.I. °British Standards Institution.

B.S.P. British standard pipe thread used on metal pipes; also used for the pillar valve thread on some air cylinders.

bubble trouble Slang term for °barotrauma.

buckle A fastening for belts and harnesses; °quick-release.

buddy Diving companion.

buddy breathing Sharing one regulator mouthpiece under water.

Bulgaria Bulgarian Federation of Underwater Sports, 48 Bul. Christo Botev, Sofia, Bulgaria. Founded 1958.

bug bag Bag carried by divers for collecting crabs, lobsters, crawfish, etc.

buoy Floating object, often anchored to the bottom, used to indicate position/direction/obstruction for navigation or reference.

buoyage A system of using buoys as navigation aids. The lateral system is used in Britain, and the cardinal system in the rest of Europe.

buoyancy The assessment of floating ability of a diver or object. Floating is positive buoyancy, sinking is negative buoyancy, and doing neither is neutral buoyancy.

buoyancy compensator vest Similar to A.B.L.J., but inferior, it is a bag that is inflated (partly or fully) by means of the diver's exhaled air (CO_2), therefore useless for breathing in the case of regulator failure. Only favoured in the U.S.A. and South Pacific areas.

burst ear Name given to a form of °barotrauma in which the ear drum ruptures inwards due to excess external pressure. If this happens, the entry of cold water so near the balance

13

organs of the inner ear can give rise to nausea, vertigo, disorientation or even unconsciousness.

burst lung Resulting from excessive pressure within the lungs related to ambient pressure. Often caused by breath-holding during ascent, but sometimes due to local obstruction or a cyst within the lung.

C

cable $\frac{1}{10}$ of a nautical mile. Taken to be 600 feet.

cable-laid Rope consisting of three right-handed hawsers, twisted together left-handedly. Weaker but more flexible than standard ropes.

Cadaques' bell In 1678 a diving bell – the designer is unknown – was functioning regularly in the little Spanish harbour of Cadaques. It was about 4 m high and it enabled two Arabs to work on a wreck for about one hour. It has also been called the Catalan bell.

caisson disease Name for decompression sickness, so called because it was found in workmen working under pressure in caissons (similar to diving bells).

cam-cleat A cleat which holds a rope firmly between two cams. The greater the strain on the rope, the more securely do the cams hold. The rope is easily released when the strain is eased.

Canada Association of Canadian Underwater Councils, Box 1303, Winnipeg 1, Manitoba, Canada. Founded 1965.

cannon Big gun, certainly in use in England in 1378; issued to the Royal Navy in 1412. Last used about 1850.

capacitor A device used for storing an electrical charge which can be released very rapidly. Used in photographic electronic flash guns.

capillary 1. Very small-bore tube. **2.** The smallest blood vessels joining arteries to veins.

carbon An element which is essential to life. Activated carbon is one ingredient used to filter compressed air for breathing. It is a superb adsorbent of gases and vapours.

carbonated A liquid containing carbon dioxide dissolved in the liquid under pressure, e.g. fizzy drinks.

carbon dioxide An oxide of carbon produced by combustion or respiration. It is heavier than air, generally odourless, colourless and tasteless. It will not support life. About 0·7 to 0·85 cu. ft of carbon dioxide are produced/man/hour on the surface.

carbon dioxide poisoning Due to CO_2 (carbon dioxide) in inspired air, poor air supply or failure of absorbent in re-breather sets. Symptoms: breathlessness and panting; dizzyness; nausea; headaches; anxiety and general distress; sweating; palpitations; loss of consciousness. In ordinary air the CO_2 content is 0·03%. 3% may be breathed for several days; 6% has an effect in only 15 minutes; and 10% causes unconsciousness and death; °air purity.

carbonic acid A weak acid formed by dissolving carbon dioxide in water.

carbon monoxide An oxide of carbon formed by incomplete combustion of carbonaceous fuels. It is highly toxic, combining irreversibly with the haemoglobin in the blood and interfering with the transport of oxygen. In mild poisoning, a persistent headaches develops. Severe poisoning results in unconsciousness and death.

cardiac arrest When the heart has stopped beating. This can result from: a heart attack; drugs; electric shock; anoxia (prolonged hypoxia).

cardiac massage A means of squeezing the heart from outside the body to keep the blood circulating. Will sometimes re-start a heart that has stopped beating.

cardinal system of buoyage °Buoyage.

carotid Main arteries (2) supplying oxygenated blood to the head and brains. They have a very strong pulse.

catalyst A substance – often finely divided metal – which assists, initiates or speeds a chemical reaction, without itself being consumed in the process.

cathode Negative electrode.

C-card A card certifying that the holder has received a certain amount of diving training (U.S.A.).

centimetre (centimeter) Unit of length being one hundredth of a metre (meter).

central nervous system The brain and spinal cord.

centroid The centre of breathing pressure, which is found 19 cm inferior and 7 cm posterior to the sternal notch.

cerebral hypoxia °Hypoxia, cerebral.

chalk A sedimentary rock. Calcium carbonate. It is used to prevent stickiness of rubber and neoprene surfaces; °French chalk.

chamber A pressurized metal container used for compression, re-compression or de-compression.

charcoal An impure form of carbon formed by heating wood or bones in the absence of air. As activated carbon, it is a useful filter medium for compressors.

charging clamp Device for connecting a high-pressure hose to an air cylinder. Also used on regulators.

charging pressure (CP) The maximum pressure to which a cylinder may be charged for normal use. Should *not* be exceeded, even by the legendary 'plus 10% to allow for cooling'.

Charles's Law (Gay Lussac) If the pressure is kept constant, the volume of a given mass of gas will vary directly as the absolute temperature.

chart A map of the coast and the sea bottom, including depths of water. Essential for navigation at sea.

chart datum The plane from which heights and depths are measured. Chart datum is set at a level below which the tide seldom falls. It approximates to the level of the lowest astronomical tide.

Chile Federacion Chilena de Deportes y Estudios subacuaticos, Casilla de Correo No 188, Santiago, Chile. Founded 1957.

chlorine A green gas used to kill germs in swimming pools. It is used at

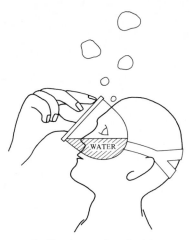

8. Clearing mask: principle

extremely small dilutions.

chloroform An anaesthetic gas. It is liquid at room temperature, and is sometimes used as a solvent for perspex (acrylic).

chokes A serious form of °decompression sickness.

Churchill, Owen Los Angeles yachtsman. Bought °de Corlieu fins in Tahiti in 1938. Obtained a licence from de Corlieu and patented his own improvements. He sold 946 pairs in 1940, and manufactured 25,000 for Allied frogmen and swimmers during World War II.

circuit training A regimen for physical fitness.

circulation The network of blood vessels, arteries, arterioles, capillaries, venules and veins, through which the blood travels.

clam cleat A cleat which holds a rope firmly between two shaped, grooved

arms. The greater the tension, the tighter the rope is held, yet it is easily released by reversing the direction of strain.

Clark, Dr Eugenie Noted American ichthyologist. Director of the Vanderbilt Oceanographic Research Station, Florida. Author of *Lady with a Spear*.

Clarke, Arthur C. Full-time American author of fiction and non-fiction. Though his subjects are mainly science fiction and space travel, he has also written many books about the underwater world, e.g. *The Coast of Coral*.

claustrophobia An obsessional neurosis characterized by fear of small spaces or of being shut in. Sometimes dangerous to divers in wrecks and in conditions of zero visibility. Panic is the great danger.

clearing ears Equalizing the pressure on each side of the ear drum by

9. Clearing mask: practice

yawning, swallowing, or the °Valsalva manoeuvre.

clearing mask Blowing water out from a flooded mask by exhaling air through the nose; °ill. 8 and 9.

clearing tubes Clearing the water from the regulator tubes and mouthpiece by exhaling air, pressing the purge valve, or holding the mouthpiece up above the first stage.

closed circuit Breathing apparatus in which the exhaled gases of respiration are re-circulated to be cleaned of carbon dioxide and re-charged with oxygen; °open circuit.

clothing °Dry suits; °wet suits.

clove hitch A knot which is commonly used for attaching a rope to a spar or bollard.

C.M.A.S. Confédération Mondiale des Activités Subaquatiques (the World Underwater Federation) An international association of diving federations and clubs.

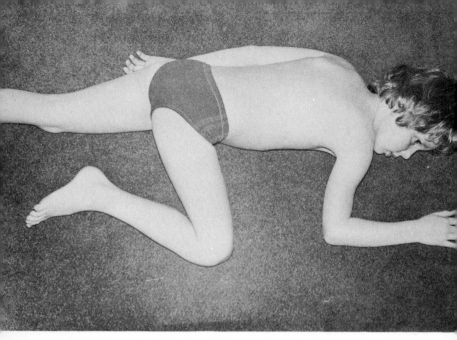

10. An unconscious but breathing patient should at all times be placed in the coma position, even during transport to doctor or hospital

C.N.S. °Central nervous system.

CO₂ Scientific shorthand for (strictly speaking) one molecule of °carbon dioxide. In diving terminology, it refers to carbon dioxide in general.

cold infections An infection of the nose and respiratory passages. The profuse mucus secretions can block the sinuses and Eustachian tubes, making diving painful or even dangerous.

cold temperature °Hypothermia.

colic A digestive upset, usually due to gas; °divers' colic.

colour Sensation received by the eyes, caused by radiations of light of different wavelengths. Under water colours fade as the water itself absorbs the colour. Red goes first; at a depth of only 1 m red is fading. At 10 m, reds are virtually absent, while orange and yellow are fading. At only 20 m, virtually the only colour present is a fairly uniform blue-green. This does not mean that colour is absent underwater, only that the depth of the water prevents you seeing it. If an artificial light source is taken under water – a torch or flash gun, for example – you will be able to see the colours once again where the light falls on them. This is why underwater photographers so frequently use artificial illumination of some sort; °colour triangle; °ill. 11.

colour triangle The effects of adding together lights of different colours. Blue + green + red = white. Blue +

green = cyan. Blue + red = magenta. Green + red = yellow. Red, blue and green are primary colours; cyan, magenta and yellow are secondary colours.

coma A state of unconsciousness. The patient is totally without sensation or response; °unconsciousness.

coma position The position in which *all* unconscious persons should be placed as long as they are breathing. They must also be transported or carried in this position, with one exception – a fractured spine; °ill. 10.

communicate The means by which divers communicate with each other under water or above, via rope signals, surface cover to shore, shore to surface cover, etc. It includes arm signals, ropes, torches (for night diving), etc.

compass 1. A device for drawing circles. **2.** A magnetic instrument used

WATER SURFACE

1 metre (3 feet)	red fading
10 metres (33 feet)	red absent orange and yellow fading
20 metres (66 feet)	only blue-green left

11. How colours are absorbed by water

12. Compass

13. Condert's diving apparatus

for determining the direction of North; nowadays calibrated in 360° in a clockwise direction; °ill. 12.

compensator Dent or facility in a face mask to enable the diver to seal his nostrils when clearing his ears.

complemental air °Inspiratory reserve; °lung volume.

compressor Mechanical device using external power to compress air. This is usually done in a number of stages, with interstage cooling and final filtration of the air.

concentration cell corrosion This occurs on metal when the formation of anodes or cathodes is due to differences in the environment, e.g. in crevices between gaskets, under deposits and scale, etc. It is usually associated with stagnant conditions. It may lead to pitting. Oxygen (dissolved in the water) accelerates corrosion: $2\,Fe + 2\,H_2O + O_2 - 2\,Fe\,(OH)_2$. Iron goes into solution at the anode; oxygen is reduced at the cathode. Further oxidation is probable converting $2\,Fe\,(OH)_2$ into $2\,Fe\,(OH)_3$. High pO_2 is, of course, normal within aqualung cylinders. Chloride ions (found in sea water) tend to migrate toward corrosion areas. This stimulates and accelerates corrosion in these areas. Corrosion pits typically appear and are autocatalytic.

concrete Engineering material consisting of a hydraulic cementing substance, aggregate and water. Sometimes iron rods are added as reinforcement. Strong in compression, weaker in tension. Concrete will set under water, which makes it a useful underwater engineering material.

condensation Small droplets of water often in the form of mist, which forms when moist air comes into contact with a cold surface.

Condert, Charles Worked as a diver in the East River, Brooklyn, New York, up to 1832. He used a free-diver apparatus, independent of surface air. He was drowned in the East River in August 1832, probably because of a malfunction in his suit; °ill. 13.

constant volume lifejacket Original name of the °A.B.L.J.

constant volume suit A dry suit in which nips or squeezes are prevented by air pressurization, and over inflation is prevented by pressure relief valves. The inflation can be provided straight from an air cylinder or, as is often the case, through a regulator connection.

contact lens An eyesight correction lens worn inside the eyelids and in contact with the conjunctiva (surface of the eyeball).

contamination The presence of harmful impurities, e.g. oil, in compressed breathing air.

contents gauge A gauge which indicates the pressure of air inside a cylinder. Simple calculations will give the volume of air left in the cylinder; °ill. 14, 15 and 16.

continental shelf Region of relatively shallow water (down to 600 feet or 200 metres) surrounding each continent. It forms a definite shelf.

contrast Visual effect due to strong differences in luminance, reflection or colour. One of the more important means of visual communication under water.

conversions (random examples):
Miles to kilometres $\times \frac{8}{5}$
Kilometres to miles $\times \frac{5}{8}$
Miles to nautical miles $-\frac{1}{8}$
Nautical miles to miles $+\frac{1}{7}$
psi to atmospheres $\div 14\cdot7$
or $\times 0\cdot068$
Ats to kilos/cm^2 = the same
°F to °C $- 32 \times \frac{5}{9}$
°C to °F $\times \frac{9}{5} + 32$
psi to feet (fresh water) $\times 2\cdot31$
psi to feet (sea water) $\times 2\cdot25$
Metres to feet $\times 3\cdot28$
Litres to pints $\times 1\cdot76$

convulsions Sudden violent uncontrolled muscular contractions due to unusual brain activity.

cord-tex Rapid-burning fuse (virtually instantaneous) used with explosives (23 ft or 7 m Cord-tex burns in 0·001 seconds); °safety fuse.

Coriolus effect Geostrophic effect; the deflection of winds and currents due to the rotation of the Earth. Deflection is to the right in the northern hemisphere, and to the left in the southern hemisphere.

Corlieu, Louis de Developed a prototype rubber foot fin in 1929. French patent dates from 1933.

coronary 1. The blood vessels supplying the heart muscles. **2.** Coronary thrombosis. A blood clot in one of these vessels, preventing efficient muscle contraction (a heart attack).

corrosion The eating away of metal by chemical action, particularly oxidation, e.g. iron – rust. Classification: galvanic corrosion; pitting; intergranular corrosion; stress corrosion; dezincification. Uniform corrosion and pitting are the most common and

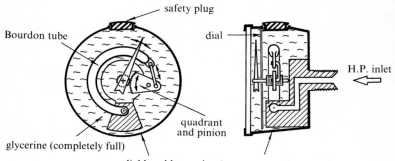

14. Contents gauge in pliable case

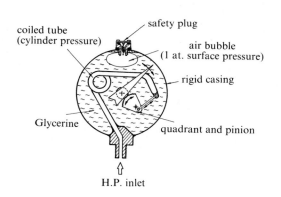

15. Contents gauge in rigid case

most damaging forms of corrosion found in high-pressure air cylinders.

Costa Rica Asociacion Costarricone de Actividades Subacuaticas, Apartado 6678, San Jose, Costa Rica. Founded 1968.

counter The part of the stern over-hanging the stern post.

Cousteau, Commander Jacques-Yves With Emile Gagnan, he perfected the modern regulator (1942–3). A Frenchman, he is probably the best known diver in the world and is deservedly called the 'father of

16. Contents gauge

modern diving'. His book *The Silent World* describes the beginning of diving as we know it today.

cox (coxwain) The man who steers the boat. In a small boat he is also in command.

C.Q.R. Very efficient pattern of anchor shaped like a plough. Holding power almost twice that of °fisherman anchor. Very reliable except in shingle; °anchor; °anchor size; °anchor warp; anchoring.

crab An edible crustacean characterized by having its abdomen reduced and carrying it permanently tucked up under its thorax.

crab hook A simple metal crook used for easing a crab from a crevice. It often damages the crab.

crack With reference to an air cylinder, to open briefly a cylinder tap or valve, so that a short burst of air escapes. Sometimes used as a general term for opening or turning on a cylinder valve.

cramp Painful seizure of one or more muscles. Usually brought on by cold, poor circulation, or unusually hard or sudden muscle contraction. Treatment: stretch muscle.

crown The knob by which a watch is wound or its hands are moved.

crustacea A class of the phylum 'arthropoda'. Mainly marine. Includes crabs, lobsters, etc.

cryogenic Very low temperature aqualungs which operate on liquid air (air liquifies at high pressures and low temperatures). Unfortunately oxygen boils at −183°C and nitrogen at −196°C; this causes trouble when producing breathable air mixtures.

crystal The transparent window through which the face of a watch is seen.

Cuba Comision Nacional de Actividades Subacuaticas, Direccion de Organismos Internacionales, Minrex, Havana, Cuba. Founded 1965 as the Federacion Cubana de Caza Submarina.

current Movement of water in a fairly defined direction.

C.V.L.J. Constant volume lifejacket. Dated term for °A.B.L.J.

cyclone Meteorological conditions of low atmospheric pressure. Generally means bad weather.

cylinder A strong metal container for compressed air. Also called a tank or bottle. May be made from steel, steel alloy, or aluminium alloy; °scuba pack; °ill. 52.

cylinder capacity The amount of air a cylinder or tank contains when it is fully charged; °ill. 17.

cylinder markings Essential marks impressed on the collar or neck of the cylinder, or the body. Usually contains information such as: manufacturer's mark and serial number, month and year of pressure test, charging pressure or working pressure and test pressure, water capacity, cylinder specification, etc.

cylinder pressure The pressure to which the air in a cylinder must be com-

pressed to achieve maximum capacity; °ill. 18.

cylinder testing Cylinders for compressed air are tested by the manufacturer. However, they should be retested at specified intervals which vary from country to country, e.g. in Britain the law requires that a cylinder be tested every five years. Most authorities consider this insufficient for diving cylinders and one recommendation is that they have a visual inspection annually, and a hydraulic test 3 years after manufacture and every two years thereafter.

Czechoslovakia Czecho-Slovak Divers Federation, Opletalova 29, 116 31, Prague 1, Czechoslovakia. Founded 1968.

CAPACITY OF CYLINDER	
Cubic Feet	Litres
40	1132
45	1274
50	1414
55	1557
60	1698
65	1840
70	1981
75	2123
80	2264

17. Cylinder capacity

lbf/in²	MN/m²	ats	bars
1800	12·4	120	122
2000	12·8	135	137
2250	14·4	150	153
2500	16·0	165	168
2650	16·9	175	179
3000	19·2	200	204

18. Cylinder pressures

D

Dalton's Law (of partial pressures) In a mixture of gases, the pressure exerted by each is equivalent to its proportion of the whole.

Danforth anchor Also called a stockless anchor, it is noted for its reliability and holding power. Unreliable on shingle; °anchor.

datum °Chart datum.

Davis, Sir Robert H. One of the giants of underwater innovation. British. Working for the famous diving firm Siebe, Gorman, Sir Robert developed many improvements to diving helmets and submarine escape hatches. He was knighted following the escape from a wrecked submarine – the *Poseidon* – of the crew using D.S.E.A. (Davis Submarine Escape Apparatus)

in 1931. Author of *Deep Diving and Submarine Operations*.

dead air space The space containing air in the respiratory system without permitting gaseous exchange, e.g. nasal passages, pharynx, trachea, etc.

deafness Either difficulty in hearing or inability to hear. Various kinds of deafness may result from °barotrauma.

Deane, John An Englishman. Patented an apparatus for working in a smoke-filled atmosphere in 1823. It was later used for diving operations with some adaptions. It incorporated a helmet and suit; °ill. 19.

decanting The act of transferring air from one cylinder to another at a lower pressure, and allowing the

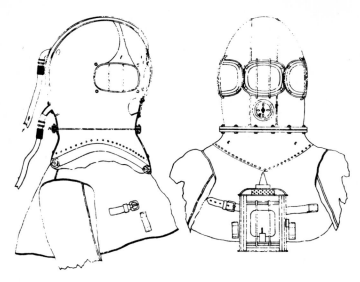

19. Deane's specification No. 4869, AD 1823

pressure differences alone to effect the transfer.

decimetre (decimeter) Unit of length: 10 cm or $\frac{1}{10}$ m.

declination The North-South alignment of a magnetic compass.

decompression The escape of dissolved gases, principally nitrogen, from the tissues in accordance with their partial pressures. A drop in pressure.

decompression meter An instrument carried by the diver which is supposed to compute time(s) and depth(s) so as to indicate absorbed nitrogen and any necessary stage decompression. It is designed to allow for repetitive dives.

decompression sickness A crippling, sometimes fatal affliction caused by bubbles of nitrogen forming in the blood and/or tissues, including the joints. Caused by incorrect decompression, usually after too rapid an ascent, or too deep or too long a dive. General symptoms: itching of skin; joint pains; numbness of limbs; chest pains; giddiness. Variously called the chokes, niggles, staggers, etc. Pain is present in 90% of cases. Paralysis affects not more than 5%.

decompression tables Published details of stages required for decompression from a large range of depth/time combinations. Usually published by the navies of the world. *None* are 100% proof against decompression sickness. (The U.S.N. considers an incidence of 5% acceptable – and this does occur, even when the tables are followed to the letter. The tables published by the Royal Navy are more conservative, and thus safer). °No-stop times; R.N.P.L. Decompression Tables.

decompression, therapeutic Treatment by planned recompression and careful, controlled decompression of a diver suffering from decompression sickness. Special tables are used.

demand valve °Regulator.

demisting Means of resisting or delaying condensation of water as mist on the inner surface of a mask face plate. Usually achieved by maintaining a wet surface by the use of a wetting agent, e.g. saliva. An oily surface is difficult to demist without using a detergent.

Denayrouze, Lt Auguste French Navy officer. With Rouquayrol, he invented a semi-independent diving apparatus – the aerophore – in 1865. It is widely regarded in many ways as the ancestor of modern scuba equipment.

Denmark Dansk Sportsdykker Forbund, Postboks 173, 1005 Copenhagen, Denmark. Founded 1965.

density 1. Mass per unit volume. **2.** Opacity. The density of a gas varies in accordance with its pressure, and increased density affects turbulent flow of air (°specific gravity). The increase of density with depth reduces maximum breathing capacity by 50% at 30 m (100 ft), 75% at 180 m (600 ft). Equipment resistance will also increase with density.

depression Meteorological term used to indicate region of lower than average atmospheric pressure. Weather is generally worse in a depression.

depth Distance from the surface of the water to the bottom.

depth compensated regulator Regulator incorporating a small orifice and working like an °R-reserve.

depth gauge An instrument which works by pressure changes, indicating depth. At the surface it registers zero, unless adjusted to include pressure of the atmosphere. Most common types are Bourdon and capillary (bathymeter); °ill. 20.

derelict Anything forsaken or thrown away by owner at sea, e.g. a forsaken vessel; °flotsam; °jetsam; °ligan; °wreck.

descent Maximum rate of descent permitted (according to Royal Navy tables) is 30 ft/10 m per minute.

desiccant A chemical which has a strong affinity for water. Used to dry air delivered by a compressor. Also in underwater camera housings to keep internal air dry and less liable to condensation, e.g. Silica gel, activated alumina.

detergent A cleaning agent with an affinity for both oil and water. Used to remove oil from articles. By removing oil, oil-suspended sediment is also removed. Modern household detergents contain whitening and foaming agents. The ability to foam has nothing to do with the detergent power.

detonator Small structure containing an easily exploded compound. This compound is relatively unstable, and can be detonated by electricity, a flame or a blow.

deviation The amount by which a magnetic compass needle deviates from North due to nearby iron, steel, or other magnetic material; °inclina-

20. Depth gauges: Bourdon type *(above)* and capillary *(below)*

tion; °variation; °declination.

dewpoint The temperature to which air must be cooled, at constant pressure, in order to become saturated, and below which precipitation of moisture occurs.

dezincification Selective solution and leaching of zinc from an alloy, e.g. brass. It leaves brittle and porous copper and copper oxide behind.

diabetes Sugar diabetes (*diabetes mellitus*) is a disease due to failure of the hormone insulin to balance correctly the intake/use of sugar in the body. An imbalance leads to irrational behaviour and unconsciousness, often without much warning. Diabetics should never dive without seeking medical advice.

diaphragm A flexible partition. **1.** Muscle between thorax and abdomen, used in the mechanics of breathing. **2.** Rubber or neoprene sheet which is the pressure sensitive part of a regulator, and which operates the air control valve.

diastole The resting dilating part of the cycle of movement shown by the heart. Blood pressure in the arteries during diastole is 70–80 mm of mercury; °blood pressure; °systole.

differences, tidal Any difference in time or height of high or low water at a given port when compared to another port.

diffusion Movement of molecules in a liquid or gas from a region of high concentration to a region of lower concentration; spreading out.

diluent Substance used to dilute another substance, e.g. nitrogen dilutes oxygen in air.

dilution hypoxia °Hypoxia, dilution.

Diolé, Philippe French journalist and one of the earliest underwater archaeologists. Author of *4,000 Years Under the Sea*.

disorientation Inability to tell the direction of 'up' or 'down'.

displacement The water pushed aside by a body in water – usually a boat. A measure of the weight of a vessel. All vessels displace water at rest and at slow speed; at high speeds some ride on the surface of the water and are said to 'plane'. Maximum efficient speed of a displacement hull is

$$1 \cdot 5\sqrt{\text{length of boat in feet}} = \text{knots}$$

or $2 \cdot 72\sqrt{\text{length of boat in metres}} = $ knots.

distress – international signals Rule 31 of the International Regulations for preventing Collisions at Sea. Red flare or orange smoke, International signal flags N & C, Morse letters SOS sent by sound, lamp or flag.

distress – diving signals Diver waving arm or hand from side to side; use of thunderflash under water (re-call).

ditching The act of abandoning in the water or throwing overboard equipment. 'Ditch and recovery' is a common scuba training drill.

diuresis A flow of urine. Head-out immersion produces a striking diuresis.

diurnal Daily tides. One high water and one low water tide a day. Generally found in or near the tropics.

dive Any one immersion by a diver beneath the surface which can be counted towards decompression time. Time measured from descending until leaving the water is commonly recorded, but decompression time is only measured until the point of leaving the bottom.

dive marshal A person in overall charge of any diving expedition (British term).

dive master A person in overall charge of any diving expedition (American term).

diver A person who has completed all his basic training, although frequently and incorrectly used of any person who is using, or has used, scuba gear.

diver's colic Abdominal pain due to to the expansion of air/gas in the stomach or intestines. The gas may be swallowed or generated by bacteria. The pain appears as a result of surfacing.

diver's marker buoy A surface buoy attached by a line to a diver to indicate his position to his surface cover or boat; a vital but much neglected piece of safety equipment. Sometimes called a 'blob buoy'.

dividers Geometrical instrument used to measure distances on charts.

diving bell Container large enough for at least one person. Open at the bottom, the internal pressure is always the same as the ambient water pressure. The earliest method of taking man under water.

diving flags International flag 'A' (I have a diver down, keep well clear and at slow speed) is recognized throughout most of the world and by the World Underwater Federation. U.S.A. diving flag; used almost exclusively in America. Nato flag 4; no longer generally recognized; °'A' flag; °ill. 21.

diving officer The person in ultimate charge of diving activities on a diving

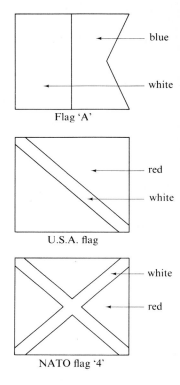

Flag 'A'

U.S.A. flag

NATO flag '4'

21. Diving flags

expedition or in a club.

dolphin kick Leg kick used in swimming and fin swimming. Both legs, held together, move vertically in an undulating movement. Virtually the only method of propulsion a diver can use if one fin has been lost.

dome port A domed covering or port through which the lens or viewfinder of a camera sees underwater. It

22. Dome ports: one for lens, the other for viewfinder

eliminates the distortion created by a flat port; °ill. 22.

Donald Duck One of the names given to the high pitched speech of divers breathing helium.

D.O.T. Department of Transportation. Authority responsible in the U.S.A. for the regulations concerning cylinder manufacture and use.

downstream A valve mechanism which operates with the opening gas. It is held closed by a powerful spring. It sometimes becomes more difficult to open as the pressure falls; °balanced;

°upstream; °ill. 23.

draught Boating term meaning the distance vertically from the water surface to the lowest point on the keel of a boat.

Drieberg, Friedrich von German inventor of a diving apparatus called the 'Triton', 1808. Triton contained an air tank or cylinder, but this was filled via a surface line. The diver carried a container in which a candle was kept alight by pumping air to it; °ill. 24.

drift Boating term meaning a move-

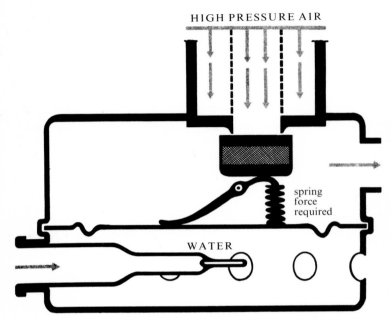

HIGH PRESSURE AIR

spring
force
required

WATER

23. Downstream valve in a single-stage twin-hose regulator *(U.S. Divers)*

ment to leeward caused by current/ tide-stream.

drift diving A dive in which the diver allows the tide-stream or current to move him over the bottom. Movement is often faster than unaided swimming and much ground can be covered, but the diver is not himself in command. Good surface cover is essential.

drinking Alcoholic drinks and diving do not mix. Alcohol promotes body heat loss, adds to the problem of nitrogen narcosis – even if 'residual' from the night before – and ruins any fine judgement. Any feeling of warmth or well-being is purely subjective. Fizzy or carbonated drinks should not be consumed before a dive; °diver's colic.

drowning Death due to immersion in water. Asphyxia is the prime cause, but three types of drowning are recognized. **1.** 'Dry' drowning – in

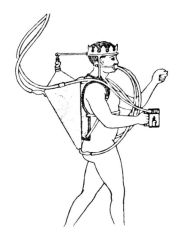

24. Drieberg's 'Triton' apparatus

20–40% of cases, no water enters the lungs – simple asphyxia causes death. **2.** 'Wet' drowning with inhalation of fresh water: the water is absorbed by the blood, leading to rupture of the blood cells and probably ventricular fibrillation by the heart; death is rapid. **3.** 'Wet' drowning with inhalation of sea water: water passes *from* the blood into the lungs; some salt enters the blood; the heart action fades slowly, taking up to 8 minutes to stop.

drugs Substances which, when absorbed by the body, alter its physiology in some way. Most have some effect on a diver's performance, e.g. asprin speeds chilling. Many seasickness drugs cause drowsiness; °alcohol.

dry suit Diving suit in which diver is kept dry and water is prevented from entering. Liable to squeeze at depth. If suit is badly torn, the suit may 'flood' badly and a disastrous loss of buoyancy may occur; °hypothermia; °wet suit; °constant volume suit.

duck dive Surface dive involving bending the waist and straightening the legs vertically. The weight or pressure of the legs then drives the diver under. Also called a jack-knife dive.

duck's beak valve A simple non-return valve consisting of two flaps of rubber. Common as the exhalation valve of some twin-hose regulators. Also called a spear valve.

Dugan, James American author and underwater historian, he assisted °Dumas and °Cousteau in preparing *The Silent World.* Accompanied Cousteau on many expeditions. Author of *Man Explores the Sea.*

Dumas, Frederic One of the pioneers of modern diving. Has worked closely with °Cousteau. Noted underwater archaeologist; author of *Deep-Water Archaeology.*

duration The time-scale of a dive for decompression purposes. It is measured from the time of leaving the surface until the moment of leaving the bottom.

Dutchman's log A means of estimating the speed of a boat: 1. throw a floating object ahead and to one side of the boat; 2. time the period required for the boat to pass the object from stem to stern; 3. calculate the speed (*a*) accurately: speed in knots =
$$\frac{\text{length of boat in feet} \times 360}{\text{time in seconds} \times 6080}$$
(*b*) approximately: speed in knots =
$$\frac{\text{length of boat in feet}}{\text{time in seconds}} \times \tfrac{1}{2}$$

E

E.A.D. °Equivalent air depth.

E.A.R. Expired air resuscitation.

ear The sense organ responsible for both hearing and balance; °ear clearing.

ear clearing The act of equalizing the air pressure in the middle ear with ambient pressure. May be achieved during a descent by: yawning; swallowing; positive muscle action (requires practice); and the °Valsalva manoeuvre. During ascent no positive action is normally needed.

eardrum Tympanum; the membrane separating the outer ear from the middle ear. It is important that every effort is made to keep it undamaged and intact. Minor perforations will usually heal unaided within 14 days, but medical advice must always be sought; °ill. 25.

ear plugs Rubber plugs are often used by swimmers to prevent the entry of water into the outer ear. Their use in any form of underwater swimming (even a foot or so below the surface) is *dangerous* and could lead to pain, bleeding and rupture of the eardrum, because the pressure of the water will drive the plugs into the ear; °reversed ears.

ears A diving term for the painful condition resulting from inability to clear the ears.

ears, reversed °Reversed ears.

ebb-tide A falling tide; the tide going out; the opposite of flood.

E.C.G. Electro cardiogram. A record of the electrical activity of the heart. Used in the diagnosis of heart disease.

echo sounder Instrument for measuring depth of water by timing the echo off the bottom, from a pulse of sound originating within the echo sounder.

ecology The study of living organisms in their own environment, divided into: **1.** Autecology, the study of a single organism in its environment; **2.** Synecology, the study of one environment and its associated organisms.

edema °Oedema.

Edgerton, Harold E. Professor of Electrical Measurements at M.I.T. in the U.S.A. Inventor of the electronic flash photographic light. Developed robot electronic flash cameras to photograph the depths of the ocean, e.g. at 25,000 ft in the Romanche Trench, equatorial Atlantic, in 1956.

E.E.G. Electro encephalogram. A record of the electrical activity of several parts of the brain. Useful in detecting abnormal activity such as could result from a °barotrauma.

effects of pressure The commonest effects of pressure are primarily movement and/or change in volume. Changes in solubility of gases, speed of transmission of sound, viscosity and density of a gas, etc.

Ekman spiral A diagram showing the deflection of wind-driven currents with increasing depth due to °Coriolis effect.

electricity Form of energy. Passage of electricity through flesh can do damage. Water, especially salt water, facilitates the passage of electricity.

electronic flash Strobe; a powerful flash of light produced by a high-voltage discharge across a gas, e.g. xenon. Of great value for photography; °ill. 26.

elimination (of nitrogen) The removal of dissolved nitrogen from the blood after a dive on compressed air. Most is eliminated within 6 hours, but complete elimination takes 12–15 hours.

embolism Blockage of blood vessel(s) as a result of pulmonary °barotrauma.

emergency ascent An ascent precipitated by a crisis or predicament. It usually entails the diver(s) having to surface as soon as possible or feasible, e.g. regulator failure; °assisted ascent; °buoyant ascent; °free ascent.

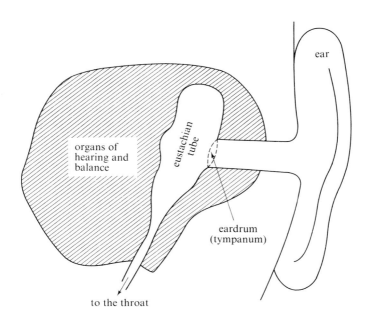

ear

organs of hearing and balance

eustachian tube

eardrum (tympanum)

to the throat

25. Eardrum and Eustachian tube

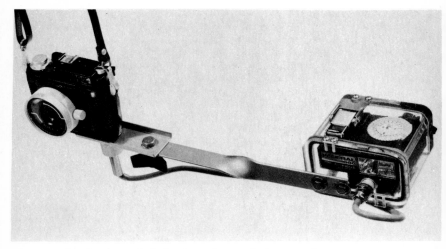

26. An electronic flash unit *(right)* attached to an underwater camera

emphysema Escape of air bubbles (gas) into the tissues as a result of pulmonary barotrauma; °interstital emphysema; °mediastinal emphysema.

entry The actual point (on shore or boat) from which the diver(s) disembarks into the water; the method of entry into the water itself – a number are taught: forward vertical entry, forward roll, and backward roll are the safest and most common.

epilepsy A disease characterized by convulsions and unconsciousness. Epileptics should not dive.

equalize The act of equalizing the pressure of air in two spaces, e.g. ear clearing; decanting.

equipment Apparatus necessary or useful for underwater swimming.

equivalent air depth Depth used for calculating decompression when diving with oxygen/nitrogen mixtures other than air, e.g. 60% oxygen – 40% nitrogen – actual depth 27 metres = E.A.D. 21 metres; decompress as for 21 metres on air.

erosion corrosion A combination of corrosion and mechanical wear. Valves, pumps, etc. often fail from this cause.

ethanol Ethyl alcohol C_2H_5OH.

ethmoid sinus °Sinus.

eupnoeic pressure The particular pressure of air under water which gives the most comfortable breathing. It depends on the position of the regulator in relation to the lungs; °centroid.

Eustachian tube Conical tube connecting the middle ear to the naso-pharynx (back of the throat); °ill. 25.

evaporation The loss of molecules from the surface of a liquid. Hastened by increased temperature and air movement. Evaporation removes heat – a vital factor where wet divers are subject to hypothermia/exposure.

exercise tolerance test Test of physical fitness. Absolute minimum standard. After stepping on to a chair 5 times in 15 seconds, the pulse should return to normal within 45 seconds.

exhaust 1. Burnt fuel gases from an internal combustion engine; not healthy to breathe and should be well away from the air intake of compressors. **2.** The air exhaled by a diver. **3.** The part of a regulator through which exhaled air passes into the water.

expedition Correctly, a dive at a new or distant location, but often used to describe a group of divers in operation.

expiratory reserve Supplemental reserve; the air in the lungs, apart from the amount usually breathed, which can be forcibly expired; °lung volume.

expired air resuscitation Currently the most efficient method of resuscitation; artificial respiration. Air from the rescuer's lungs is blown into the patient's lungs through nose/mouth. The patient must have an open airway, achieved by tilting the head well back and pulling the jaw forward.

exposure Caused by cold, wet and wind chill. A grave risk to life; °hypothermia; °water chill; °wind chill.

exposure, photographic The quantity of light required to produce a correct image on the film. Depends on lens aperture, shutter speed and film speed.

extension The act of opening the airway of a person needing resuscitation, achieved by tilting the head well back and pulling the jaw forward.

eye The organ of the sense of sight. Not usually affected by barotrauma, although a 'bent' eyeball has been recorded by a wearer of contact lenses. Vision is, however, affected by the refractive index of water, which is greater than that of air.

F

face mask A piece of equipment that always encloses the nose and eyes, and also (in a full face mask) the mouth. The body is usually of rubber and the front – the face plate – is of clear perspex, acrylic or glass. The latter, for safety's sake, should be of toughened or laminated glass. The face mask provides a pocket of air between eyes and water, enabling the eyes to see under water; °compensator; °ill. 27, 27a, 28, 28a.

Falco, Albert This Frenchman is one of °Cousteau's closest associates, accompanying him and his research vessel *Calypso* on nearly all their expeditions.

fainting Unconsciousness, usually brief, due to temporary inadequacy of the blood supply to the brain. There are often several factors contributing to a faint, including: (a) hyperventilation; (b) sudden assumption of an upright posture; (c) increased intrapulmonary pressure; (d) breathing pure oxygen – particularly under pressure; (e) anxiety; (f) after-effects of alcohol; (g) hunger; (h) pain; (i) incubation of a febrile illness; (j) fatigue; (k) sea sickness; °syncope.

fairway Boating term meaning the navigable part of a river, estuary, harbour, etc.

Faeroes Islands Faroese Underwater Federation, Vardagota 27, 3800 Torshavn, Faeroes Islands. Founded 1957.

fatigue, metal All compressed-air cylinders undergo repeated load cycling, i.e. they are repeatedly pressurized and depressurized. These are ideal conditions for metal fatigue failure. Steel cylinders will fail if the pressure is high enough, but if the maximum pressure is reduced, usually to below half bursting pressure or less, fatigue failure will not occur, however many load cycles are applied. Aluminium cylinders will fail in time, whatever the maximum pressure. However, if this maximum pressure is kept to about $\frac{1}{4}$ burst pressure, the fatigue life would be about 100,000,000 cycles, or a daily charge for 300,000 years. Most

aluminium cyclinders are designed for a life of 200 years or 100,000 charges. It is not quite true, however, to say that steel cylinders have an indefinite life while aluminium cylinders have a finite one. Other factors such as the fact that steel is prone to rust and various forms of corrosion to which aluminium is impervious have to be taken into account. Both forms of cylinder are safe, provided they are never charged above their recommended working pressure; °corrosion.

fathom Measure of water depth: 6 feet or 1·83 metres.

felt pad Used in compressor filters to retain the particulate active ingredients. Has some value in removing large solid particles from the air stream.

fender Resilient object (often an old car tyre) hanging over the side of a boat to prevent damage in the event of bumping into a quay, etc.

F.F.E.S.S.M. Fédération Française d'Etudes et de Sports Sousmarins. The French national federation.

'F' flag A single hoist means: I am disabled, communicate with me.

filter, air Fine pore substance to remove all traces of oil, water, solids and odours from breathing air. Fitted to the outlet of an air compressor, it may contain: felt pad(s); activated charcoal; silica gel; molecular sieve; activated alumina, etc.

filter, light Coloured glass or gelatine used to absorb or reduce the transmission of some colours while allowing others to pass freely, e.g. a yellow filter absorbs (darkens) blue light, but lets red and green light pass through; °colour triangle.

27, 27*a*, 28, 28*a*. Face masks various types *(Typhoon)*

Finland Federation of Finnish Sports Divers, Topeliuksenkatu 41a, 00250 Helsinki 25, Finland. Founded 1956.

fins Extensions to the feet to increase the power of propulsion of swimming. There are two types in general use: full-foot fitting, which makes the fin virtually an extension of the foot; and strap fitting, in which the heel is open; °de Corlieu; °ill. 29 and 30.

first aid Medical assistance given to sustain life; prevent worsening of any condition; promote recovery. Resuscitation and the stopping of bleed-ing are the most important; °cardiac massage; °E.A.R; °sea sickness; °shock.

first stage Where the reduction of air pressure by a regulator is split into stages, the reduction from air cylinder pressure to about 150 psi takes place in the first stage. In a single-hose regulator, the first stage is attached to the cylinder and the °second stage is located in the mouthpiece; °ill. 31.

fish Aquatic vertebrates. They are cold-blooded, covered in scales and breathe by means of gills. Whales and dol-

39

29. Fin with open heel and strap fitting

30. Fin with full-foot fitting

phins are *not* fish – they are mammals.

fisherman anchor The traditionally shaped anchor. Holds on most bottoms and is better than °Danforth or °C.Q.R. on stone; °anchor size; °anchor warp.

fish-eye A photographic lens with an extremely wide angle of view of approximately 180°; °ill. 32.

fish ring A device used by spearfisher-

men for holding their catch while swimming.

fitness Precise levels of fitness are debatable, but it is generally agreed that diving and snorkelling require at least average and preferably above-average physical fitness. Alcohol, tobacco, illness, disease and obesity all adversely affect physical fitness.

fixe-palmes Fin grips; rubber anchor straps used to prevent fins slipping off the feet; °ill. 3.

flag Coloured material, usually bunting (wool), flown singly or with others as a visual signal; °'A' flag; °diving flags; °'F' flag; °ill. 21.

flames A means of indicating distress when no other means is available.

flare A coloured burning chemical that gives an intense light for visual signalling, including distress.

flash point The temperature at which a volatile inflammable substance gives off sufficient vapour to produce a flash when a flame is applied.

Fleuss, Henry An early diving engineer who worked with °Davis. Developed an oxygen rebreathing device in 1879, testing it at the old Polytechnic, Regent Street, London. It is the ancestor of many modern safety devices and firemen's respirators.

float °Diver's marker buoy.

floating Any object which stays on the surface of any body of water without any other means of support; °Archimedes' Principle; °buoyancy.

flooding When the air-spaces in a piece of equipment fill with water. A °floodtide in progress.

floodtide A rising or incoming tide.

flotsam Floating material, usually man-made or wreckage. Not animals or

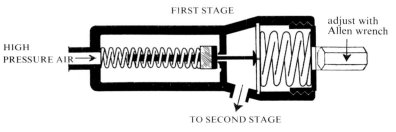

STANDARD SINGLE HOSE
FIRST STAGE

HIGH
PRESSURE AIR →

adjust with
Allen wrench

TO SECOND STAGE

31. A standard first stage of a single-hose regulator *(U.S. Divers)*

32. Top view of an underwater camera fitted with a fish-eye lens in a dome port housing, which is why two convex surfaces are visible

plants; °derelict; °jetsam; °ligan; °wreck.

flow meter Instrument for measuring the rate of flow of a liquid or gas.

fluorescence The property of many substances of absorbing light of one wavelength and emitting light of another wavelength. Thus the substance appears to be unnaturally bright.

flushing The active movement of water within a wet suit, and its replacement by colder water from outside. A loose fit at neck, waist, wrists or ankle, oversize suits, bad zips and flexing during exertion, all increase flushing.

flutter kick The leg stroke characteristic of crawl swimmers.

flying To avoid decompression sickness, no flying above a cabin altitude of 5,000–9,000 ft (1,500–2,700 m) is permitted for: 2 hours after a 'no-stop' dive, or 24 hours after a dive involving stoppages. If decompression sickness has developed, no flying above a cabin pressure of 1,000 ft (304 m).

F.N.R.S. 2 and 3 French-built bathyscaphes. F.N.R.S. 2 damaged during unmanned dive, 1948. F.N.R.S. 3 reached 13,287 ft (4,045 m).

fog Small droplets of condensed water in the atmosphere. Visibility less than 3,280 ft (1,000 m). In a dense fog, visibility is less than 164 ft (50 m). Visibility exceeding the above distance but less than good may be due to mist or heat haze, depending on circumstances; °ill. 33.

following sea A sea that overtakes or tends to overtake a vessel. There is danger of pooping and/or broaching; °pooped.

Forel-Ule scale Judgement of watercolour by comparison with prepared standards containing differing proportions of copper sulphate, potassium dichromate and cobalt sulphate

Code	Description	Definition	
0	Dense fog	Objects not visible at	50 yards
1	Thick fog	,, ,, ,, ,,	1 cable
2	Fog	,, ,, ,, ,,	2 cables
3	Moderate fog	,, ,, ,, ,,	$\frac{1}{2}$ mile
4	Mist or haze or very poor visibility	,, ,, ,, ,,	1 mile
5	Poor visibility	,, ,, ,, ,,	2 miles
6	Moderate visibility	,, ,, ,, ,,	5 miles
7	Good visibility	,, ,, ,, ,,	10 miles
8	Very good visibility	,, ,, ,, ,,	30 miles
9	Excellent visibility	,, ,, ,, ,,	30 miles

33. Fog and visibility scale for ships at sea

34. Freminet's diving suits

solutions. 22 shades, from blue, through green and yellow to brown, are recognized.

foreshore The part of the shore between high- and low-water marks.

formaldehyde HCHO. Gas which, when dissolved in water, is widely used as a preservative for fish (for study or display – not for eating); °formalin.

formalin A 40% solution of °formaldehyde.

foul air Term used for contaminated breathing air, especially that with taste or smell; °oil.

four-stroke cycle Internal combustion engine using the Otto Cycle of ♦ induction ♦ compression ♦ power ♦ exhaust.

France Fédération Française d'Études et des Sports Sous-marins, Siège Social 24, Quai de Rive-Neuve, 13007 Marseille, France. Founded 1948 as the Fédération des Activités Sous-Marines.

free ascent Ascent with air in the lungs but without the further use of an aqualung. It is usually an emergency ascent when a regulator fails. It may also be a buoyant ascent. There is danger of barotrauma, especially embolism. There is also the danger of decompression sickness, because of the excessive speed of ascent.

free diving Term used to describe aqualung or scuba diving; in fact any diving carried out without an air hose fed from the surface.

freeze The solidifying of a liquid as it cools. Fresh water freezes at 32°F (0°C), and sea water at a lower temperature (−1·91°C) because it is saline.

Freminet,' Sieur In the 1770s, this Frenchman designed several items of diving apparatus; they did not work very well, but his would seem to be the first attempt at a true diving helmet; °ill. 34.

French chalk Powdered talc, i.e. hydrated magnesium silicate. Used to prevent rubber sticking to itself and to

43

ease the problem of rubber suits gripping or sticking when being pulled on.

frogman Term coined by the press during World War II to describe a diver wearing fins. Any diver using scuba, mask and fins.

front Meteorological term for the boundary separating two adjacent air masses of different origin.

frontal sinus °Sinus.

frostbite Serious result of exposure, where the tissues have actually become frozen and are badly damaged. Commonly or primarily affects fingers, toes, ears and nose.

full-face mask Face mask which encloses eyes, nose and mouth. Useful, in conjunction with a dry suit, for diving in polluted waters. Mainly professional applications and not much used by amateurs.

G

gage °Depth gauge; °pressure gauge.

Gagnan, Emile Co-inventor, with °Cousteau, of the regulator. They met in Paris in December 1942 and adapted a valve designed for feeding cooking gas to car engines. The prototype regulator appeared early in 1943.

gale Wind force 8 on the Beaufort wind scale. Wind speed 34–40 knots.

Galeazzi, Dr Roberto Italian submarine engineer. In 1930 he was the first person to descend to a depth of 700 ft in the sea in his 'buboscopic turret'.

galvanic corrosion When two dissimilar metals are in contact or are electrically connected and exposed to an electrolyte (electrically conducting fluid), one of them is eaten away. The anode metal is eaten away, the cathode metal is not. Copper is more likely to form a cathode; aluminium, zinc and magnesium form anodes; °sacrificial anode.

galvanize To coat iron with zinc. (Technically it could be said to mean the production of electricity by using two dissimilar metals.)

gas A state of matter where the molecules move freely in space, always occupying the whole of the space available.

gas analysis °Air purity.

gaseous exchange The process which takes place in the alveoli of the lungs when the blood gives up carbon dioxide and takes up oxygen.

gas equation For a perfect gas (derived from °Boyle's and °Charles's Laws):

$$pv = nRT$$

where p = pressure in ata
v = volume in litres
R = Universal Gas Constant
T = absolute temperature
n = moles

gas laws °Boyle's; °Charles's; °Dalton's; °gas equation; °Henry's; °Van der Waal's equation.

gasoline Petroleum spirit; petrol.

Gay Lussac °Charles's Law.

geostrophic effect °Coriolus effect.

German Democratic Republic Tauchsportclub der DDR, 1272 Neuenhagen-Berlin, Langenbeckstrasse 36–39, German Democratic Republic.

German Federal Republic Verband Deutscher Sporttaucher e.V., D-2000 Hamburg 36, Bleichenbrucke 10, German Federal Republic. Founded 1954, although two clubs – Süddeutsche (1950) and Deutscher Unterwasser Club (1952) – are older.

Gilpatrick, Guy American author. Experimented with basic equipment in the 1920s and 1930s. His book *The Complete Goggler* is probably the first on sports diving.

gland 1. An organ of the body producing secretions. 2. A seal round a rod or in a pipe to prevent leakage, usually of a liquid.

glottis The opening at the upper end of the trachea or windpipe.

goggles Primitive aid to underwater vision that covers only the eyes. Subject to squeeze with increased depth and should be used only by surface swimmers, *never* for underwater use.

Great Britain British Sub Aqua Club, 70 Brompton Road, London SW3 1HA, Great Britain. Founded 1953. The Sub-Aqua Association, 28 Southampton Street, London WC2.

Greece Hellenic Federation for Underwater Activities, Agios Kosmas, Glyfada, Athens, Greece. Founded 1952.

grid An arrangement of lines at 90° to form squares. Used in searching, measuring and surveying under water.

Guernsey Island Blue Dolphin Sub-Aqua Club, Castle Emplacement, The Cottage Grange, Praye Road, Vale, Guernsey, Channel Islands.

Gugen, N. Oscar Founder, first member and first chairman of the British Sub Aqua Club (1953).

gun metal An alloy of copper and zinc.

gunwale The upper edge of the side of a vessel.

H

haemoglobin The pigment in red blood corpuscles which can combine reversibly with oxygen, by picking it up in the lungs and releasing it in the tissues. Unfortunately, it combines more strongly with carbon monoxide when exposed to it.

Haldane, Prof. J. B. S. Son of John S. °Haldane. British. Continuing his father's work, he became a world authority in the field of decompression and °decompression tables.

Haldane, Dr John Scott Father of Prof. J. B. S. °Haldane. British. Made tremendous advances in the field of decompression research. He proposed to the British Admiralty that they set up a commission to study diving. The committee was formed the following year, 1906. Author of *Life at High Pressures*.

Halley, Dr Edmund Famous English astronomer, after whom Halley's comet was named. In 1720 he developed a large diving bell that was supplied with air from empty casks dropped on a line from the surface; °ill. 35.

35. Halley's diving bell being supplied with air from a barrel

halocline Horizontal boundary between waters of different salinity.

hand bearing °Bearing, hand.

hand spear Hand-held spear used for catching fish; °Hawaiian sling.

harassment Technique of causing the unexpected to happen. Used on trainees to see how they cope with emergencies, etc. A popular technique in the USA and Europe, but little-used in Britain.

harbour Shelter on the coast for the mooring of vessels, and for loading and unloading. There are usually local laws controlling the use of harbours, especially with regard to vessels' speed. Before diving in a harbour, it is essential to inform the harbour master.

harness A device for holding the scuba or aqualung on the back. It usually consists of a metal band and webbing straps, and is fastened by a °quick-release buckle; °ill. 36 and 52.

harpoon A spear with a barbed point. May be propelled by hand or gun.

Hass, Dr Hans Viennese underwater scientist, photographer and author. He first ventured underwater with a camera in the Caribbean in 1939. His first book, *Diving to Adventure*, set new standards. His wife, Lotte, introduced glamour to the depths.

Hawaiian sling A simple tubular device into which a hand spear is placed. The spear is propelled by a rubber band like a catapult.

hawser-laid Rope made of three strands which spiral round each other, usually from left to right. The most common form of rope.

headache A symptom of an illness. Always seek to cure the cause of the illness, not merely the symptoms. Divers with headaches, even if alleviated by drugs, should not dive.

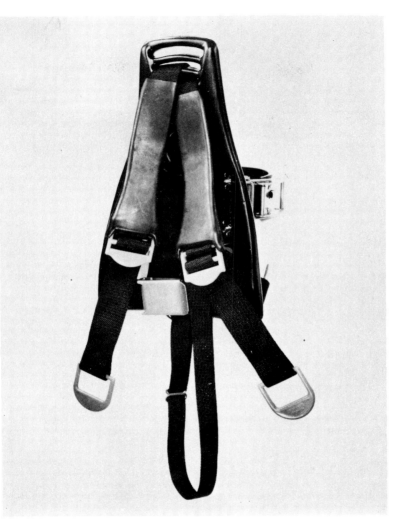

36. One of many different types of harness

head sea A sea which comes towards and meets the bow of a vessel head on.

hearing Sense which detects sound. The ears are the organs of balance as well as hearing.

heart The muscular organ located in the thorax which moves the blood round the body. The rate of contractions in adults is 60/80 per minute at rest, and up to 210 per minute during exercise. A person with heart trouble should only dive with his doctor's permission, and then only with *at least two* other buddy divers.

heart failure This occurs when the auricles fail to deal with the venous return blood. The veins near the heart distend and venous pressure rises.

heart massage First aid procedure which aims at re-starting a stopped heart. Correct massage also moves the blood along until the heart re-starts.

heat loss Heat flows from hot to cold. It travels by conduction, convection or radiation. A suited diver loses most body heat by conduction, assisted on the surface by the evaporation of water; °evaporation; °wind chill.

heat transfer °Heat loss.

heave to Boating term meaning to stop at sea without anchoring or mooring.

heel The way a boat leans sideways from the vertical.

heliox Breathing mixture using helium to replace nitrogen as the diluent; °helium.

helium Noble or inert gas sometimes used as a diluent in breathing mixtures. It has low density and diffuses rapidly, affecting heat conduction, decompression and speech. Using it intead of nitrogen removes the danger of nitrogen narcosis. Can cause high pressure nervous syndrome.

helm The tiller or wheel used to steer a vessel.

helmet The hood of a wet suit is sometimes called a helmet. More correctly, it is the metal head-covering used by the standard diver, who is sometimes called a helmet or hard-hat diver.

helmet squeeze Situation in standard diving where a sudden fall or drop by the diver increases the pressure round the diver without allowing the pressure to rise within the suit, or if the pressure within the suit suddenly drops. The diver is literally forced into his helmet, causing severe bruising and sometimes death; °nips; °squeeze.

hemoglobin °Haemoglobin.

Henry's Law The amount of a gas that will dissolve in a liquid at a given temperature is almost directly proportional to the partial pressure of that gas.

Hering-Breur reflex The termination of respiration due to stretching of the lungs. This reflex is so weak in man that for all practical purposes it is absent.

high pressure In diving terms, any pressure over 10 atmospheres. Cylinders contain air at high pressure, usually between 120 and 300 ats.

high pressure nervous syndrome When diving deeper than 500 ft (152 m) using helium as the sole diluent, the diver sometimes becomes dizzy, nauseous and has tremors which eventually result in convulsions. The replacement of some of the helium by nitrogen, to 18% of the mixture, allows dives down to 1,000 ft (300 m) without symptoms (Duke University, U.S.A.,

1973).

high water The greatest depth of water occurring daily, due to the action of the tides. Can be predicted with considerable accuracy.

Hill, Prof. Leonard One of the first scientists to study the effects of decompression in living tissues through a microscope. In 1930 he was a member of a British Admiralty committee advising on decompression apparatus. Author of *Caisson Sickness*.

history, diving 450 BC Scyllas did some underwater salvage work for the Persian King Xerxes. 415 BC Greek divers removed stakes from Syracuse harbour to allow attacking vessels to enter. 360 BC Aristotle refers to the use of the diving bell. 333 BC Alexander the Great reputed to have submerged in a diving bell. AD 1203 divers cut ships' cables at the siege of Les Andelys, France. 1535 diver explored the bottom of Lake Neni (Italy) looking for sunken barges with a suit invented by Guglielmo de Lorena. 1690 a shallow water diving dress was demonstrated in the river Thames (U.K.). 1754 a helmet suit with air pumped in was used on salvage at Yarmouth (U.K.). 1790 first modern diving bell was used in Ramsgate harbour (U.K.). 1802 William Forder developed and used a dress supplied with air pumped in by bellows on the surface. 1819 Augustus Siebe introduced his first, open, diving dress. 1825 William H. James describes a self-contained diving suit in which compressed air was stored in a metal reservoir shaped like a belt round the waist. 1837 Augustus Siebe developed the closed diving suit, the forerunner of all modern standard gear. 1866 Rouquayrol-Denayrouze developed the first satisfactory regulator for scuba; the absence of suitable high-pressure cylinders limited the equipment to surface demand use. 1877 Paul Bert completed the first real research into respiration. 1878 H.A. Fleuss (of Siebe Gorman & Co.) developed the first closed-circuit oxygen re-breathing apparatus. 1884 the first scientific diving took place by Prof. H. Milne-Edwards, in Sicily. 1893 possibly the first underwater photographs were taken at Banyuls-sur-Mer by Louis Boutan. 1893 the first recompression chamber was installed by Sir Earnest Moir for Hudson river tunnel workers. 1902, in conjunction with Fleuss, Sir Robert H. Davis produced self-contained submarine escape apparatus. 1907 the work of Dr J.S. Haldane was published, which gave tables for decompression down to 200 ft (60 m). 1918 Ohugushi respirator patented–manually controlled regulator successfully used down to 300 ft (90 m). 1924 Commander Yves le Prieur patented his scuba unit in which the air-flow was controlled manually. 1929 the first rubber foot fins marketed by Louis °de Corlieu. 1938 patent granted to Maxim Forjot of France for a mask covering eyes and nose, although other masks had been in use before this. 1942 °Cousteau and °Gagnan discussed their regulator, which received its first successful trial the following year.

histotoxic hypoxia °Hypoxia, histotoxic.

H.O.A.L. British Home Office specifications for aluminium cylinders.

Hodges, Commander H.J. One of Britain's first underwater photographers. Was taught to dive by °Dumas, and studied underwater photography under °Tailliez and °Cousteau. Did valuable work for the Royal Navy, photographing men escaping from submarines with Davis apparatus. Joined °Hass's Caribbean expedition in 1954, and was lost while diving on oxygen.

Holger Neilson A manual method of artificial respiration.

Hong Kong Underwater Federation of Hong Kong, P.O. Box 14232, Hong Kong. Founded 1967, but oldest club dates back to 1953.

hood The headpiece of a wet suit.

hookah A surface supplied diver. The first stage reduction takes place on the surface and a hose connects it to the diver-carried second stage.

H.O.S. British Home Office specification 'S' for seamless alloy steel cylinders.

hose On a twin-hose regulator, the corrugated low pressure tubes that carry the diver's breathing/exhaust air at ambient pressure, located between regulator and mouthpiece. On a single-hose regulator, a medium pressure tube working at about $7 \times$ atmospheric pressure located between the first and second stages. On a pressure or contents gauge, a high-pressure tube working at about $200 \times$ atmospheric pressure located between the cylinder or regulator and the gauge.

H.O.T. British Home Office specification 'T' for seamless alloy steel cylinders.

Houot, Commandant Georges S. Succeeded °Cousteau in the French Navy. With engineer Pierre-Henri Willm, he descended to a then record depth of 13,287 ft off Dakar in 1954, in the bathysphere FNRS-3. The story is related in their book *2,000 Fathoms Down in the Bathyscaphe*.

housing A waterproof case to enclose a camera or some other item; °ill. 37.

H.P. °High pressure.

H.P.N.S. °High pressure nervous syndrome.

hull The outside shell of a boat, consisting of the bottom and sides.

Hungary Magyar Konnyubuvar Szovetseg, 1054 Budapest Rosenberg hp. utca 1, Hungary. Founded 1968.

hydraulic test A process in which a cylinder is pressure-tested to determine whether it is suitable for continued use. By using water to pressurize the cylinder, there is no disastrous explosion if the cylinder ruptures. Most cylinders are permanently enlarged by the test. This is called the 'permanent set'. Regulations define the maximum permissible set.

hydrocarbon A compound of hydrogen and carbon, including most oils and oil products. Combustible and therefore a great risk, which increases with pO_2.

hydrogen The lightest element known. A gas which burns vigorously in air or oxygen. Despite this, hydrogen is sometimes used as a diluent for oxygen in diving to greater depths, because its narcotic effect is less than that of nitrogen.

hydrostatic An effect of non-moving

37. Housing containing *(above)* an electronic flash or strobe unit, and *(below)* a camera

water; usually a pressure effect.

hygroscopic A substance which attracts water vapour from a gas to itself. Activated alumina and silica gel are hygroscopic substances used in the filtration of breathing air from compressors.

hyper- Greater or larger than; excessive, e.g. hyperventilation – breathing in excess.

hypercapnia Excess carbon dioxide in the blood causing over stimulation of the respiratory centre. A result of breath-holding or under-breathing in an attempt to conserve air consumption. Also a result of exertion.

hyperthermia Overheating. Normal body temperature is 98·5°F (37°C); 102°F (38°C) causes lethargy; 104°F (40°C) causes permanent brain dam-age.

hyperventilation Over (deep) breathing. A dangerous practice because the process flushes carbon dioxide from the lungs. Carbon dioxide is a respiratory stimulant and deep breathing removes the urge to breathe, even under hypoxia conditions; unconsciousness and drowning can follow; °hypoxia, latent.

hypo- Smaller or less than; below the normal value of.

hypoglycaemia Condition in which the level of sugar in the blood falls below normal (c. 100 mg%) and the brain is affected. One of the conditions found in diabetes when a diabetic has either missed a meal or has exerted himself more than usual. Symptoms: restlessness; sweating; double vision; coma.

Treatment: administer sugar, chocolate, sweet drinks, etc., if conscious; if unconscious, glucose will have to be administered in hospital.

hypothermia Reduced body core temperature (below 95°F or 35°C). Death occurs by 88°F (31·5°C). Shivering starts at 97°F (36·5°C) and stops at 91°F (33°C). Symptoms: feeling cold; mental and physical lethargy; mental confusion; slurred speech; shivering; stiffness, pain, cramp in muscles; abnormal vision and unconsciousness – the latter two are the most serious. Infants, diabetics and the aged are especially susceptible. Treatment: prevent further heat loss; immerse the trunk in warm water at 108-113°F (42-44°C). All treatment should be under strict supervision, if possible. Latest research indicates that mild hypothermia might increase the effects of nitrogen narcosis. Alcohol, spiced foods, etc. actually increase heat loss, despite subjective feeling of warmth; °after drop; °temperature core; °water chill; °wind chill.

hypoxia Shortage of oxygen, sometimes incorrectly called °anoxia; °syncope.

hypoxia, anaemic Hypoxia due to the inadequate transport of oxygen by the blood, e.g. due to blood disease, carbon monoxide poisoning, or circulatory failure.

hypoxia, anoxic Hypoxia due to insufficient pO_2 in inspired air, a fault in °mixture breathing.

hypoxia, cerebral Actual shortage of oxygen in the brain. The product of all other forms of hypoxia. The result is unconsciousness.

hypoxia, dilution A hazard of closed-circuit re-breathing aparatus. The counter lung becomes filled with nitrogen only from the tissues of a diver who was recently breathing air. The danger is minimized by flushing the lungs with pure oxygen and exhaling to the atmosphere for a few minutes before diving. (Full lungs contain 4 litres nitrogen; another 400 ml is released in the first half-hour on oxygen.)

hypoxia, histotoxic Damage to the tissues of the body due to insufficient oxygen being present. The brain is particularly susceptible. Also possible in the presence of adequate oxygen when something else interferes with metabolism.

hypoxia, latent Peculiar to snorkel diving. Pressure at depth will raise an inadequate pO_2 for underwater activity. On ascent, however, the pressure is reduced and the pO_2 may fall below the level needed to maintain consciousness. While unconsciousness may be only 0·001% fatal on land, it is at least 50% fatal at a depth of 10 ft (3 m) under water – an increase in risk of death of 50,000; °hyperventilation.

hypoxia, stagnant Hypoxia due to failure of the heart or the circulation.

hysteresis A lag or delay of some kind, e.g. it may take a suction of $x+$ inches of water to start a regulator air flow which only requires x inches of water to maintain.

hysteria Mental and physical disorders of the body not of organic origin. Symptoms may include loss of memory, vision, hearing, muscle power, etc.

I

ice The solid form of water. Fresh water freezes at 32°F (0°C). Sea water freezes at a lower temperature, depending on the salinity of the water. Ice is less dense than water and so it floats. When diving under ice, safety precautions must be strict; all divers should be roped to the surface.

icing When high-pressure air expands, it cools. If the air is moist and especially if ambient temperature is low, ice can form. If this happens inside a regulator, the supply of air to the diver will be cut off. Venturi valves are particularly prone to icing in the above conditions.

inboard Inside a boat.

inclination The vertical dip of a compass needle. It points *through* the Earth straight to magnetic north.

inert gas A gas which is chemically inactive and does not combine with any other substance. The 'noble gases'

were once called the inert gases, but it is now known they can form compounds; °argon; °helium; °krypton; °neon; °radon; °xenon.

inflatable In boating terms, a boat, usually made of a rubberized material, which is inflated by air at a comparatively low pressure. Very resilient, stable buoyant, it makes a good dive platform and inshore rescue craft. More important for the inland-based diver, it can be deflated and packed in a car; °ill. 38.

initial suction pressure (I.S.P.) The amount of suction needed to start a flow of air through a regulator. Ideally less than 5cm water/litre air/ second (Nyman and Van der Valt); °hysteresis; °P-factor.

inland Away from the coast.

inlet valve Valve which controls the entry of a liquid or gas.

inner ear The part of the ear which is

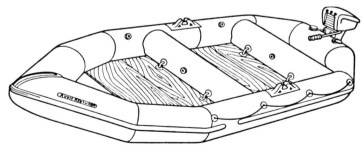

38. A typical inflatable boat

concerned with balance and interpreting sound; °ear.

inset The way in which a tide-stream tends to hug the coastline, setting in to large bays and inlets.

inspiratory reserve Complemental air. The extra air, over and above normal respiration, which can be forcibly inspired; °lung volume.

instructor A qualified person who knows how to communicate his knowledge to others, e.g. Club Instructor, N.A.U.I., P.A.D.I., moniteur, etc.

intergranular corrosion Localized attack at metal grain boundaries. Sometimes complete disintegration can occur, even when relatively little metal has disolved.

international sea scale °Sea.

interstital emphysema Air which has escaped as a result of pulmonary barotrauma, rupturing the alveoli, but remaining in the lung.

inversion Meteorological term: a layer of air in which the temperature increases with height. (Chimney smoke stays near the ground and does not rise.)

invertebrate Animal without an internal bone or cartilage backbone (vertebral column).

inverted set A scuba unit in which the air cylinders are carried or held with the pillar valve(s) down, pointing towards the ground. The main advantage is that the diver can turn his own air on/off, even when under water.

Ireland Comhairle Fo Thuinn, Morningside, Leixlip, Co. Kildare, Republic of Ireland. Founded 1963.

iron Valuable metal. Because of cor-

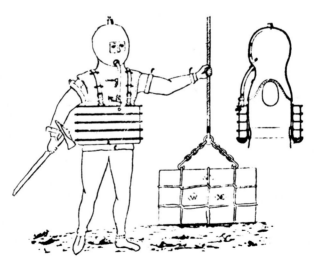

39. What may have been the first working scuba, by James

rosion problems, it is most commonly used in an alloy with other elements, e.g. with carbon in steel or with chromium in stainless steel.

isobar Line drawn on a map or chart linking places of equal barometric pressure.

isotherm Line drawn on a map or chart linking places of equal temperature.

I.S.P. Initial suction pressure.

Israel Federation for Underwater Activities, 16 Hanatziv Street, Tel-Aviv, Israel.

Italy Federazione Italiana Pesca Sportiva e Attivita Subaquei, Viale Tiziano 70, 00100 Roma, Italy. Founded 1943.

itches Localized burning or tingling itch. A blotchy marbling rash may be present. Common after short deep dives, and rare after long shallow ones. May be the only evidence or symptom of °decompression sickness, indicating no more than a too rapid decompression (Stanley Miles).

J

jack-knife A surface dive in which the body is bent sharply forward at the waist and the legs thrown into the air. Another name for a duck dive.

James, William An Englishman, James invented or developed what is possibly the first workable free-diving or scuba apparatus, in 1825; °ill. 39.

Japan Japan Underwater Federation, 1245 Kawana Ito-Shi, 414, Japan.

jellyfish A stage in the life history of some coelenterates (primitive animals). It is the stage in which the animal is sexually active. Jellyfish stings may be severe, causing pain, blistering and high temperature. Some forms can be fatal. There are no specific antidotes.

Jersey Jersey Federation of Underwater Activities, October Cottage, Route de Petit Port, St Brelade, Jersey. Founded 1967.

jetsam Goods from ships which sink and are washed ashore. Technically anything thrown overboard to lighten a vessel in danger; °derelict; °flotsam; °ligan; °wreck.

jockstrap Harness strap passing between the legs to secure the lower part of the harness. The idea is to prevent the cylinder riding up and hitting the back of the head, or the lifejacket slipping over the head.

J-reserve Also known as a constant reserve valve. A spring-loaded valve held open by air pressure until the cylinder pressure fails to a predetermined mark, e.g. 300 psi. It then closes. To obtain the remaining air, the diver has to pull a lever and mechanically open the valve. It is a physical system of informing the diver that his air supply is low.

K

kedge A second or supplementary anchor, lighter than the main one; °anchor; °anchor size: °C.Q.R.; °Danforth anchor; °fisherman anchor.

keel The lowest point on a ship. It provides longitudinal strength, and reduces yaw and heel.

Keller, Hannes Swiss mathematics teacher. With the assistance of Albert Buhlman, physiologist and cardiac specialist at the University of Zurich, he developed a combination of gases that would enable divers to reach great depths with safety. In 1959 he dived to 400 ft in a lake. Later, with *Life* magazine editor Kenneth MacLeish, he reached 725 ft in Lake Maggiore in safety. In 1962, with British journalist Peter Small, he descended to 1,000 ft off Catalina Island, California. An accident threw the delicate gas mixture out of balance and Peter Small died.

kelp Collective term for seaweeds of the laminaria genus. In Britain, so much kelp grows that from mean low water spring tides to about 60 ft (20 m), varying with water clarity, reference is often made to the 'kelp forest'. The kelp forest is a vital part of some sub-littoral ecologies, providing much food, shelter and anchorage.

Kendall, Henry W. American. Joint author, with Hilbert Schenck Jr, of one of the first authoritative books on underwater photography *(Underwater Photography)* in 1954.

Kessler, Franz A German who produced, in 1616, a diving bell that was independent of lines to the surface. It descended with weights and jettisoned them to surface. It was in advance of its time but was not developed further; °ill. 40.

kiss of life Popular term for °expired

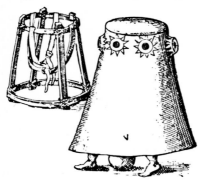

40. Kessler's 'free' diving bell

air resuscitation, whether mouth to nose or mouth to mouth.

Klingert, Heinrich German inventor of several items of diving equipment in the 1790s: one was a diving suit, another a hydrostatic lift; °ill. 41 and 42.

43. Knife

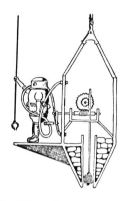

41. Klingert's hydrostatic lift

42. A diving suit designed by Klingert

knife Considered to be a vital item of diving equipment, primarily for cutting lines in the event of a diver becoming snagged underwater; °ill. 43.

knot **1.** The speed of one nautical mile per hour (approx. 1·7 feet/second or 0·5 metre/second). **2.** A method of joining or securing ropes. There are many different knots and some of them are of particular value to divers, e.g. °bowline.

K-valve A non-reserve valve. A simple on/off valve with no reserve mechanism. Popular with British divers, who invariably use a cylinder contents gauge and so do not require a physical reserve.

L

laminar flow The movement of a fluid (e.g. air) advancing in separate sheets or laminae. A gentle low-velocity flow through a straight tube is laminar – the molecules in the centre move more rapidly than those at the periphery. In relation to the human respiratory system, it is said (Miles) that flow rates below 20 litres/minute are largely laminar; °Reynold's number; °turbulent.

latent hypoxia °Hypoxia, latent.

lateral system of buoyage °Buoyage.

latex A soft form of rubber; the milky fluid of the rubber plant.

latitude The angular distance in degrees North or South of the Equator. Parallels of latitude are scribed on all maps or charts. By definition, one minute of latitude equals one nautical mile.

launching The procedure of causing a boat to float on water.

law There are many laws, in every country, which directly or indirectly affect divers, e.g. Britain's Protection of Wrecks Act 1973, but there are too many to mention here and in any case they vary too often by repeal, innovation, etc. There are some laws of physics that can universally be taught or explained: °Boyle's Law; °Charles's Law; °Dalton's Law and °Henry's Law.

learning Research has shown that a student retains no more than 20-30% of the material he hears in a lesson or lecture. Retention is increased if he can see the material he is being taught. 75% of what we learn is due to sight; 15% is due to hearing; the 10% remainder is due to other senses, including touch.

lecture A means of passing information on from one person to many. It is a one-way system and the lecturer is not aware of the degree of either comprehension or retention. Most diving instruction systems or methods include lectures; °lesson.

lee Boating term meaning the sheltered side, away from the wind; °windward.

leeward Boating term: towards or on the side sheltered from the wind.

leeway Movement of a boat by the wind. Corrections for leeway must be made if a vessel's track is to be plotted correctly.

Le Prieur, Commandant Yves French Navy. Developed a self-contained diving suit in 1926. The 'Fernes-Le Prieur' owed something to the Rouquayrol-Denayrouze principle, and was further developed. When de Corlieu flippers were added in 1935, the combination produced the first true free-diver.

lesson The passing on of information from one person to another in which (*a*) both persons actively participate and (*b*) there is 'feedback' from the pupil(s) so that the teacher does not progress until previous lessons have been learned; °lecture.

44. Lethbridge's salvage apparatus

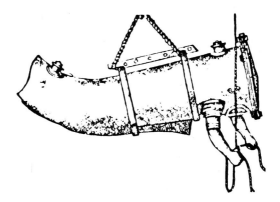

Lethbridge, John In 1715 this Englishman took out a patent for a 'Diving Machine'. A combination of diving chamber and armoured suit, Lethbridge carried out salvage down to depths of 50 feet in it; °ill. 44.

Liechtenstein Tauchclub Bubbles Liechtenstein, Ramschwagweg, F1-9496 Balzers, Principality of Liechtenstein. Founded 1971.

lifejacket A buoyant device designed to keep the face out of the water and the wearer afloat. Surface lifejackets (S.L.J.'s) may contain buoyant material, or may be inflatable by mouth or gas cylinder. A diver should wear an °A.B.L.J.

lifeline A line connecting a diver to another diver or more usually to a tender on the surface. The lifeline must be firmly attached to the diver. A diver-to-tender lifeline is essential when only one diver is in the water – particularly in water with low visibility – or when diving under ice.

life-saving Techniques evolved by various organizations to enable swimmers or divers to rescue swimmers/divers in danger of drowning.

lifting When lifting objects under water, it is usual to use buoyant vessels. These may be rigid or flexible, and are usually inflated or filled with air while under water. During the lift, the air will expand (°Boyle's Law), accelerating the lift and/or rupturing the buoyancy bag or lifting vessel unless there is some means for the excess air to escape.

ligan Anything sunk, but buoyed in order that it can be re-located; °derelict; °flotsam; °jetsam; °wreck.

limiting line An arbitrary line drawn across decompression tables separating dive schedules which carry minimal risk from those which carry unacceptable (for sports divers) risk.

line, safety °Lifeline.

Link, Edwin American millionaire who made his fortune with the Link aviation trainer. He became an enthusiastic underwater historian, and in 1950 sold his firm and purchased a trawler for diving. With his wife,

Link has carried out much work of an archaeological nature. In 1964, he developed an inflatable rubber submersible dwelling called 'Spid'. Two divers lived in it for nearly fifty hours. It was a success, although too small for long-term habitation.

litre (liter) A metric unit of capacity or volume. There are approximately 28 litres in one cubic foot. One litre of fresh water weighs exactly one kilogram.

l'ivresse des grandes profondeurs Cousteau's original description of °nitrogen narcosis. Translation: rapture (or intoxication) of the great depths.

log book A book in which a record is kept of time, location and depth of every dive, together with other interesting or important information. Commercial divers in Britain are required by law to maintain a log book.

longitude The angular distance measured from the meridian through Greenwich, England. Usually expressed in degrees°, minutes and seconds East or West.

Longley. Dr W. H. American ichthyologist at the Carnegie Institute marine research station in the Dry Tortugas, Florida. Carried out valuable underwater photographic work, commencing in the Caribbean in 1917. He was one of the first to use colour – French autochrome plates – under water.

low pressure In diving, any pressure under 10 atmospheres or bars (150 psi).

low visibility A matter of relativity. In general, underwater visibility of less than 6 ft or 2 m may be called low, but in areas of normally marvellous visibility, three times this distance might be termed low.

L.P. Abbreviation for °low pressure.

lubricant, grease Common lubricants are basically hydrocarbons – compounds of hydrogen and carbon. They are inflammable, especially in conditions of high pO_2. Where high-pressure air or oxygen is concerned, only silicone greases can be used and even then only sparingly.

lubricant, oil Air compressors are highly stressed machines requiring adequate lubrication. Some lubricants can get into the breathing air if the filter is inefficient, and mineral oils in particular can cause severe lung irritation and oedema. Vegetable oils are supposed to be less irritant, but they are also less efficient lubricants. Most oil companies have produced special oils for these purposes.

lung An organ of the body used for gaseous exchange. An abbreviated term for aqualung (scuba).

lung volume For the average man: inspiratory reserve 2,000 ml; tidal volume 500 ml; expiratory reserve 2,000 ml (these are termed 'the vital capacity'); residual air 1,500 ml. Total volume 6,000 ml.

Luxembourg Fédération Luxembourgeoise des Activités et Sports Sub-Aquatiques, Case postale No 53, Luxembourg-Ville, Luxembourg. Founded 1963.

M

magnetic north The point near the north pole towards which a magnetic needle will point. In fact, the direction of magnetic north varies over the surface of the Earth and moves slowly, so that it is in a different place each year. Magnetic variation should, therefore, be clearly indicated on any chart, together with annual changes.

magnetic rubber Magnetic flexible material used in the preparation of visual aids.

magnetometer An electronic device for measuring local magnetic flux. This varies with rock strata or wrecks in the vicinity and is, therefore, a valuable search tool.

maintenance Minimizing the effects of time and wear on equipment. Most diving equipment repays washing with clean fresh water and drying in a gentle heat. Avoid prolonged ex-posure to sunlight, salt or oil.

Maiorca, Enzo Italian holder of the depth record unaided by breathing apparatus. On 18 August 1973, he dived to 265 ft (81 m) clad in a wet suit but no mask, fins or breathing apparatus. The dive lasted 2 minutes 18 seconds.

making Tides are said to be 'making' when their range is increasing towards spring tides; °taking off.

Malta Malta Sub Aqua Club, c/o F. Valletta, 10 Brighella Street, Hamrun, Malta. Founded 1955.

manifold A high-pressure connecting pipe between two or more air cylinders; °ill. 45.

manilla Manilla hemp is a fibre from a plant of the banana family grown in the Philippines and tropical America. Ropes made from manilla are strong, water-resistant and resistant to rub-

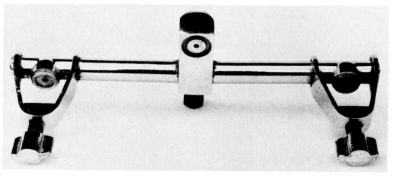

45. Manifold for connecting two cylinders or tanks

marker buoy

bing. Minimum breaking strain for half-inch (12·7 mm) circumference rope is 280 lbs (127 kg).

marker buoy A (usually) small buoy used to indicate the position of some object on the bottom. Not a navigation buoy; °diver's marker buoy.

Marx, Robert F. American underwater archaeologist and historian. Has carried out excavations at Port Royal, etc. Author of *They Dared the Deep* (1968). Underwater archaeologist for the Government of Jamaica.

mask °Face mask.

mask squeeze This happens when the face plate is squeezed against or towards the face with increasing pressure (increasing depth). This effect is due to °Boyle's Law on the air space. Severe cases can give rise to a bleeding nose, congested eyes and even black eyes. Snorting or breathing into the mask through your nose will prevent mask squeeze.

maturity onset obesity °Obesity which appears gradually with the onset of middle age. It is due to decreasing energy output without a corresponding decrease in food intake. The increased layer of fat can to a certain extent make a diver less prone to cold, but unfortunately fatty tissue is more prone to decompression sickness.

maxillary sinus °Sinus.

mechanical advantage The ratio of the actual load raised to the force applied. In pulleys, this is always less than the velocity ratio, due to friction losses. Without friction, mechanical advantage = velocity ratio.

mediastinum The space in the thorax between the lungs and behind the sternum. The heart lies in the medias-

tinum.

mediastinal emphysema A form of °interstital emphysema in the °mediastinum. Air may also rise into the neck, where it 'crackles'.

medical disqualification Diving is not normally permissible with the following ailments/defects: gross °obesity; impaired exercise tolerance; perforated eardrum; tuberculosis; lung cysts; lung surgery; spontaneous pneumothorax; emotionally induced asthma; ischaemic heart disease; aortic systolic murmur; diastolic pressure over 100 mm mercury; proteinurea; insulin-requiring diabetes; epilepsy. This is almost certainly not a complete list.

medical examination An examination for fitness to dive. It should cover: heart, lungs, ears and sinuses, and any °medical disqualification.

mercury A heavy, poisonous metal which is molten at normal temperatures. Mercury is *extremely* hazardous in contact with aluminium and will eat it away quite rapidly.

metabolism The chemistry of the body. It is divided into anabolism or building up, and catabolism or breaking down.

metal detection One can use a magnetic compass for close, large ferrous objects, but it is more common to use a °magnetometer, a highly sensitive electronic device, for measuring variations in the Earth's magnetic field.

metre (meter) Metric unit of length: approximately $39\frac{1}{2}$ inches.

metric system Decimal measuring system, the standard or basic units of which are: metre (length), gram (weight) and litre (volume).

Prefixes used include:

mega (M) × 1,000,000
kilo (k) × 1,000
deci (d) ÷ 10
centi (c) ÷ 100
micro (μ) ÷ 1,000,000

Abbreviations include:

millimetre (mm)
centimetre (cm)
metre (m)
kilometre (km)
litre (l)
gram (g)
kilogram (kg)

Meyer-Overton theory There is a parallel between the solubility of a narcotic in fat and its narcotic effect. The more soluble it is in fat, the less soluble it is in water and the more potent it is as an anaesthetic (1899, 1901). Oil/water solubility at 37°C (approx. 99°F):

Helium   1·7:1   mild narcotic
Neon   2·1:1   mild narcotic
Hydrogen   3·0:1   increasing narcosis
Nitrogen   5·2:1   increasing narcosis
Argon   5·3:1   increasing narcosis
Krypton   9·6:1   increasing narcosis
Xenon   20·0:1 anaesthetic

Mexico Associacion Mexicana de Actividades Sub Acuaticas, Calzada de Tacubaya 249-401, Mexico 11 D.F.
Mickey Mouse °Donald Duck.
middle ear The part of the ear concerned with amplifying sound vibrations. It is air-filled and connected to the pharynx by the °Eustachian tube. The air responds to °Boyle's Law and, therefore, the ear needs care when diving. The middle ear may be pres-

surized to prevent rupture of the tympanum as pressure increases with depth.
Miles, Surgeon Admiral Stanley Royal Navy. Author of *Underwater Medicine* (1962).
millibar (mb) $\frac{1}{1000}$ part of a bar. Used to indicate surface atmospheric pressure in weather broadcasting. In fact it varies, e.g. in Britain the atmospheric pressure at sea-level ranges between 960 mb and 1040 mb.
millimetre (mm) $\frac{1}{1000}$ of a metre.
Milne, John Scottish teacher of architectural and mechanical drawing in Edinburgh. In 1828 he published a pamphlet of a plan for raising vessels which had been sunk in deep water. It utilized air buoys.
miniflare A flare which consists of a cartridge which may be ignited by a percussion cap. Special holders are available for striking the percussion caps. Flares, stars and smokes are available in various colours.
minimum breaking strain The least load under which a new rope is liable to break.
minute volume The total volume of air passing in and out of the lungs in one minute. This varies from person to person and with the degree of their activity, but for a diver at the surface it is estimated to be: 1 cu ft (25 l) per minute.
mist °Fog.
mixture breathing Breathing oxygen diluted other than with nitrogen to 80%. Common diluents used are: nitrogen in some other proportion, hydrogen and helium. By using such mixtures, the onset of nitrogen narcosis can be virtually eliminated. De-

compression schedules alter with mixture. Mixture diving is a job for the professional or scientist and is rarely used by club divers; °H.P.N.S.

molecular sieve Synthetic crystaline zeolites (active sand). Agents of selective adsorption, which are extremely efficient agents for drying and purifying compressed air. Expensive. Have a preference for water and will lose efficiency unless gas is pre-dried by silica gel or activated alumina.

Monaco Club Chasse et Exploration Sous-Marine de Monaco, 30 rue Grimaldi, Monaco. Founded 1951.

moniteur A word of French origin meaning instructor. Through the C.M.A.S. it is now an international qualification, with one, two, three and four star moniteurs. Equivalence is given to other national schemes. Examinations are taken for the first three stars, but the fourth is awarded by appointment.

monofilament A synthetic thread, e.g. nylon, which has usually been produced by extrusion. It is in effect a long, thin, flexible, solid rod.

Monro effect The use of shaped explosives to increase the directional effect, e.g. 'punches' a hole through the object to which it is attached. Using 5 lbs explosive and 6 ins stand-off, the impact effect is 24×10^5 lbs of explosive. Ratio of diameter to length is about 1:2. The liner has an angle of 45°, and the air stand-off distance is $2 \times$ the diameter.

motion sickness °Antihistamine; °sea sickness; °travel sickness.

mouthpiece This is the point where the compressed air of the aqualung (scuba) enters the diver's body. The common mouthpiece is a thin flange which fits outside the teeth but inside the lips. Two protrusions inside the mouthpiece are held by the teeth. This keeps the teeth apart and the mouthpiece secure.

mouth to mouth °E.A.R.

multiple dives When more than one dive takes place within a few hours, allowance has to be made for residual nitrogen left by the earlier dive(s). Decompression schedules must be modified. The Royal Navy schedule for repeat dives is: for dives shallower than 140 ft (42 m), no penalty if 6 hours elapse on the surface between dives; if less than 6 hours elapse, decompression must be for the total time of both dives to the maximum depth achieved on either dive; deeper than 140 ft, only one dive is allowed in every 24 hours.

N

narcosis To render insensible. Particularly an adverse affect on the nervous system of any substance, e.g. alcohol, many drugs and nitrogen under pressure; °nitrogen narcosis.

narcotic Any substance which clouds the consciousness, causes sleepiness or changes the way in which the brain is working. Common narcotics: °narcosis; °nitrogen narcosis.

narks Popular term or abbreviation for °nitrogen narcosis.

nasal Appertaining to the nose.

N.A.U.I. The National Association of Underwater Instructors, one of the leading American associations of professional instructors of sports divers. Address: 22809 Barton Road, Colton (Grand Terrace), California 92324.

nausea Sensation of sickness; feeling of imminent vomiting. Symptom of °foul air poisoning or °sea sickness.

nautical mile One minute of latitude. This varies over the surface of the Earth, but is standardized as 6,080 ft (1853 m) (its value at 40° latitude).

navigation The science of knowing (*a*) exactly where you are, (*b*) where you have been, and (*c*) determining the way to go. The most useful navigation aids are a sextant, a compass and a chart.

neap tide Tide with the least range between high water and low water, occurring roughly every 14 days, 7 days after a spring tide.

necrosis Death of bone or tissue; °aseptic bone necrosis.

negative buoyancy Being heavier than water and, therefore, sinking.

neon Noble gas (lately called an 'inert' gas). Sometimes used as a diluent in breathing mixtures. North Sea Ocean Systems (U.K.) have used neon/oxygen mixtures to dive down to 520 ft (158 m). They claim this shortens decompression times, while eliminating °Mickey Mouse speech.

neoprene A synthetic rubber much favoured for diving because of its resistance to chemical, salt, oil and sun corrosion. Foam neoprene is the material used to make most wet suits.

nervous system The rapid communication system of the body, consisting of: sense organs (skin, eye, ear, etc.); sensory nerves; central nervous system (brain, spinal cord); motor nerves; and motor organs (usually muscles).

Netherlands Nederlandse Onderwatersport Bond, Balistraat 96, Den Haag, Netherlands. Founded 1962, although several clubs are much older.

Newton (N) °S.I. unit of force, producing an acceleration of 1 m/s² when acting on a mass of 1 kg.

New Zealand New Zealand Underwater Association, 30 Orakei Road, Remuera, Auckland, New Zealand. Founded 1954.

niggles Very mild pain in the limbs; a minor form of decompression sickness.

night diving Diving at night with torches is popular because of the emergence of nocturnal animals and the different appearance and behaviour of various animals. Special precautions should be observed, including: **1.** every diver should possess some means of artificial illumination such as a torch or illuminated flasher, which is attached to him via a line or clip; **2.** a shore beacon or similar marker to indicate the direction of return; **3.** agreed light signals, e.g. *O.K.* (two short flashes, repeated several times) and *distress* (a continuous beam waved from side to side).

nips Squeezes. A painful squeeze where a dry suit containing air is compressed with depth, trapping a fold of suit and consequently skin. Pressurizing the suit with air prevents nips, but then special care is required during ascent.

nitrates Minerals essential for the proper growth of °phytoplankton. Availability varies with depth. Surface waters are replenished by autumn and winter storms; °plankton.

nitrogen The gas which forms 78·09% of air. It combines with other elements with difficulty, being almost inert. It gives rise to the problems of °decompression sickness and °nitrogen narcosis.

nitrogen narcosis Effect similar to drunkenness caused by nitrogen in the body under pressure. Symptoms: increase in confidence; loss of muscular control; 'drunkenness'; apprehension; poor comprehension; unconsciousness. *Note:* Individuals vary in their susceptibility, and even in individuals from day to day. Effects do not usually become serious shallower than 100 ft (30 m), and this may be extended to 150 ft (45 m) with training and experience. If affected, rising to the surface will always alleviate the symptoms. There are no after-effects. Some scientists believe that carbon dioxide retention is either the main or a significant part of the cause of nitrogen narcosis.

nitrogen oxides Nitrogen, under certain conditions, can combine with oxygen, forming: nitrous oxide (anaesthetic or 'laughing gas'), and nitrogen dioxide and nitric oxide (these dissolve in water to form acids which are respiratory irritants, encouraging emphysema or bronchitis).

noble gas Chemically inactive gaseous element: °argon, °helium, °krypton, °neon, °radon, °xenon.

no-decompression limits °No-stop time.

non-return valve A valve which permits the passage of air/water in one direction only, e.g. in regulator mouthpieces.

normal ascent °Ascent, normal.

north The earth turns on an axis. One end of this axis is called north and the other south. The needle on a magnetic compass always points to °magnetic north, which is not exactly the same, but which lies in the same approximate direction.

Norway Norges Dykkerforbund, Postboks 6514, Redelokka, Oslo 5, Norway. Founded 1957 as the Norges Amatordykkerforbund.

nose bleed Fairly common among trainee divers, who may abuse their noses while trying to clear their ears. Easily confused with sinus bleeding, which may also occur on early dives. Treatment: rest with head forward, the nose pinched, and breathe through the mouth.

nose clip A spring clip which pinches the nose closed. This makes °ear clearing possible without using the fingers – invaluable with a full-face mask – but it makes mask clearing or ear clearing extremely difficult with an ordinary mask.

no-stop time The maximum length of dive at any given depth from which a continuous ascent may be made without stage decompression. The time is computed from the moment of leaving the surface until the moment of leaving the bottom. See page 67.

nylon Synthetic or plastic material. Used as a fibre for ropes, it is strong but has a high stretch and will melt in heat. Used as a solid material, is excellent for washers and similar items that have to withstand heavy wear.

No-stop times, R.N. (1968):				
9 m	—	30 ft	—	No limit
12 m	—	40 ft	—	135 mins
15 m	—	50 ft	—	85 mins
18 m	—	60 ft	—	60 mins
21 m	—	70 ft	—	40 mins
24 m	—	80 ft	—	30 mins
27 m	—	90 ft	—	25 mins
30 m	—	100 ft	—	20 mins
33 m	—	110 ft	—	17 mins
36 m	—	120 ft	—	14 mins
39 m	—	130 ft	—	11 mins
42 m	—	140 ft	—	9 mins
45 m	—	150 ft	—	8 mins

Note: Ascent rate 60 ft (18 m) minute

No-stop times, U.S.N. (1970):			
30 ft	— No limit	110 ft	— 20 mins
40 ft	— 200 mins	120 ft	— 15 mins
50 ft	— 100 mins	130 ft	— 10 mins
60 ft	— 60 mins	140 ft	— 10 mins
70 ft	— 50 mins	150 ft	— 5 mins
80 ft	— 40 mins	160 ft	— 5 mins
90 ft	— 30 mins	170 ft	— 5 mins
100 ft	— 25 mins		

Note: Ascent rate 60 ft (18 m) minute

No-stop times, R.N.P.L. (1975):		
9 m	—	No limit
10 m	—	232 mins
12 m	—	137 mins
14 m	—	96 mins
16 m	—	72 mins
18 m	—	57 mins
20 m	—	46 mins
22 m	—	38 mins
24 m	—	32 mins
26 m	—	27 mins
28 m	—	23 mins
30 m	—	20 mins
32 m	—	18 mins
34 m	—	16 mins
36 m	—	14 mins
38 m	—	12 mins
40 m	—	11 mins
42 m	—	10 mins
44 m	—	9 mins
46 m	—	8 mins
48 m	—	8 mins
50 m	—	7 mins

Note: Ascent Rate
15 m/minute

O

obesity Excessive fat stored in the tissues. It is almost always due to over-eating and/or lack of exercise. Gross obesity may be taken to be 20% over weight. Even 10% is too much for divers; °maturity onset obesity.

oceanography The science of studying the behaviour of seas and oceans, and the coastline.

octopus rig A system in which a second or reserve regulator is taken off the first stage of an existing regulator, providing a spare or emergency regulator.

octopush A form of underwater hockey. Two teams of six, all wearing basic equipment, use 'pushers' to move a lead 'squid' to score 'gulls'. The game originated in Britain. The rules can be obtained from the B.S.A.C.

oedema Fluid-filled tissues which become oversize. It is one symptom of °decompression sickness or of its treatment; °oil.

67

Ohugushi respirator British patent granted in June 1918. An underwater breathing apparatus or scuba; the diver obtained a flow of air by clenching his teeth and inhaled the air through his nose.

oil A lubricant which is fluid at normal temperatures, as opposed to grease, which is solid at the same temperatures. Oil vapour in inspired air will cause nausea, pulmonary °oedema and possibly pneumonia.

open circuit Where air (or some other breathing mixture) is exhausted to waste (into the water) after breathing once. The least economical, but the safest and most popular, form of scuba; °closed circuit.

open water A river or the sea, sometimes a lake. A term used to indicate diving in naturally occurring water, rather than in artificial water such as a swimming pool.

oral By mouth, or appertaining to the mouth.

orientation The ability to know where one is with respect to up, down, left, right, front, back, etc. Orientation may be confused by nitrogen narcosis or by diving out of sight of the surface or the bottom. Water seeping into the inner ear through a perforated eardrum can cause a loss of orientation and balance.

O-ring A sealing ring circular in shape and in cross-section. The most efficient and popular form of sealing for underwater apparatus.

outlet valve A one-way exit for air or water.

oxy-arc An underwater cutting torch which uses an electrical arc in a blast of oxygen. At 80 volts and 400-600 amps at a temperature of 500°C it will melt metal, which is then blown away. The gas °argon may be used instead, in which case there is no oxidation. This form of underwater cutting is both expensive and dangerous.

oxygen The element which is essential to life as we know it. It is used in the release of energy from food. The brain in particular will be irreversibly damaged if deprived of oxygen for more than approximately 4 minutes at normal temperatures. Oxygen (O_2) exists in a free state in the atmosphere, and in the atmosphere it forms approximately 21% by volume; °anoxia; °hypoxia; °oxygen consumption; °oxygen debt; °oxygen poisoning.

oxygen concentration cell °Concentration cell corrosion.

oxygen consumption This varies with the individual, but for general calculations it can be assumed that a healthy adult at rest will consume 0·25 l/min; while swimming 1·3–1·9 l/min; and a trained athlete at maximum effort 5 l/min. (1 cubic foot equals 28·3 litres.)

oxygen debt When muscles exercise vigorously, they consume more energy than the body can provide by using up oxygen. This 'borrowed' energy has to be replaced by consuming more oxygen than normal when the exercise stops. This is the reason for heavy breathing after exercise.

oxygen poisoning Oxygen when it is at a greater pressure than in the atmosphere is poisonous. Evidence suggests that this is due to direct inhibition of intra-cellular metabolism. pO_2 500–

1000 mm (which range includes pure oxygen at normal atmospheric pressure) causes chronic oxygen poisoning. At this pressure several days' exposure is generally required for the symptoms to develop: slowing of pulse; lowered pulse pressure; vaso constriction in C.N.S. and retinal vessels; fatigue; sore chest, particularly on deep inspiration; dry cough; pneumonia. At a pO_2 1500 mm, acute oxygen poisoning can develop within minutes. The symptoms are uncertain and variable, but they usually appear in this sequence: lip twitching; dizzyness; nausea; choking sensation; dyspnoea and tremor; convulsions resembling an epileptic fit. Chronic poisoning could occur in underwater habitats and/or saturation diving. Acute poisoning could occur with compressed air at 10 ata or bars (297 ft or 90 m). In all cases individual tolerance and responses vary enormously, both from person to person and from day to day. Diving on pure oxygen is nowadays limited to professional or research divers, and even then it is limited to a depth of 25 ft or 7·6 m, due to the obvious dangers.

oxygen syncope °Shallow water blackout.

P

paddleboard A floating board resembling a Hawaiian surfboard on which a spearfisherman or scuba diver can lay prone. He fins or paddles offshore to dive, returning to the float to rest or return to shore.

P.A.D.I. The Professional Association of Diving Instructors. One of the leading U.S.A. instructor training organizations for sports divers. Address: P.O. Box 177, Costa Mesa, California 92627, U.S.A.

pain Symptom of some disease, disorder or damage to the body. Alleviating the pain does not cure the cause or prevent the effects, so divers should not enter the water under the influence of analgesics.

painter Rope fitted to the bow of an open boat.

palsy °Paralysis.

Panama Club de Yates y Pesca, P.O. Box 4327, Panama 5, Panama.

panic A mental condition in which rational thought and action are impossible. In or under the water, the subject or rescuer is in danger of his life. The possibility of panic can never be eliminated, but good training is instrumental in reducing this likelihood.

Paracetamol A pain-killing drug which in excess is toxic to the liver. Death has resulted within three days of taking only 20 tablets.

paralysis Inability to move muscles. A symptom of serious decompression sickness.

Parkerize A process for reducing the incidence of corrosion inside steel cylinders. A special compound is used to fill the open pores of heated steel cylinders, leaving a thin film on the surface when the cylinder cools.

partial pressure The pressure exerted by one gas only, in a mixture of gases; °Dalton's Law.

Peau, Etienne An accomplished French naturalist, Peau was inspired by °Boutan's photographs. He took photographs in the cold, dirty waters of the Seine Bay around 1905. He developed a method of using close-up photographs in murky water. He developed a cone with a glass port at each end. The cone was filled with clean water. With the camera lens at the small end and the subject in front of the other, Peau was able to take good pictures in soup-like water.

perfect gas A gas which would obey both °Boyle's and °Charles's Laws exactly. Most gases only approximately obey these laws, and only at low pressures and at temperatures well above the temperature of liquefaction.

perforation A small hole, particularly in the tympanum or eardrum. Apart from any effect during the dive (°burst ear), the perforation may allow infection to enter and/or it may affect the hearing. Diving should cease until a doctor agrees that the hole has healed – generally from 10 days to three weeks.

performance factor °P-factor.

perspex Plexiglass. Acrylic plastic of great transparency. Easily heat-moulded and cemented. Resistant to water. Extensively used for underwater camera housings.

Peru Comision Nacional de Caza Submarina y Actividades Subacuaticas, Estadio Municipal, Tribuna Sur 3er, Casilla 2248, Lima, Peru.

petroil A mixture of petrol (gasoline) and oil, used as fuel for many two-stroke engines. Common mixtures are between 2% and 10% oil in petrol.

pewter A metal alloy based on tin. Modern pewter: 91% tin, 7·5% antimony and 1·5% copper. Pewter was first used nearly 2,000 years ago, when it contained sufficient lead to cause the surface to darken with age; °restoration.

P-factor Performance factor. A factor suggested by Nyman and Van der Valt to be used in the evaluation of regulators. It is the average suction pressure needed to achieve flow rates of: 0–1/min, 85–1/min, 150–1/min, 225–l/min, 300–l/min, and 380–l/min air flow from H.P. cylinders at 40, 90, 140 and 190 bars (ata) pressure. The average of 24 measurements 'P' should ideally be less than 5 and not more than 10 cm water/litre air/second; °I.S.P.

phosphorescence Property of shining after exposure to light. Technically, any light given out by living organisms is not phosphorescence.

photogrametry Using special photographic techniques for accurate measurement and mapping. Of great value in archaeology.

physics The study of the properties of matter and energy.

physiology The study of the functioning of living organisms and their organs.

phytoplankton Plant °plankton. The basis of all food chains in the sea.

Piccard, Auguste Swiss physicist. He

46. Pillar valve of cross-flow type

developed three °bathyscaphes for exploring deep water. The first was the FNRS–2 (the FNRS–1 was a balloon). It descended to 4,600 ft without crew in 1948. In 1953, Piccard and his son Jacques dived to 3,500 ft off Naples in the *Trieste*, the third bathyscaphe built by the Italians. Later, in 1954, the *Trieste*, with the same crew, reached 10,395 ft at the same site.

pillar valve The outlet/inlet valve of a high-pressure air cylinder; °balanced valve; °J–reserve; °K–valve; °R–reserve: °ill. 46.

pitting The formation of pits or holes in metal. It is an unpredictable process. The anode remains stationary and corrosion progresses invariably on one spot. Pitting often starts as °concentration cell corrosion, accelerating as the pit becomes a crevice,

increasing the concentration cell effect.

pivoting point Boats turn about a point approximately one third back from the bows. Thus both bows and stern move when the rudder is put over. This fact must be appreciated when a boat cover is being provided for divers in the water.

plaited Rope consisting of 8 strands or more, with or without a central core. There is less stretch and distortion than with °hawser laid rope. The strongest, least extensible and most flexible rope is probably nylon plaited round a central core.

plane A boat riding on the surface of the water rather than displacing the water; °aquaplane; °displacement.

plankton Minute animals and plants, and their eggs, spores, larvae, etc. drifting in the water. Generally occur

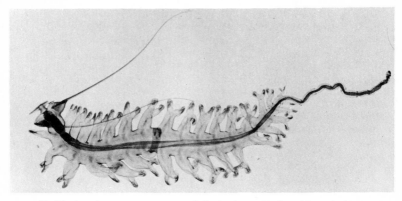

48. Planktonic worm, *Tomopteris helgolandia* (× 8), found in quite large numbers in shallow water at certain times of the year

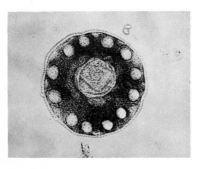

47. Plankton: egg of a marine worm. *Scolecolepidis vividis* (× 175)

near the surface of the sea. In temperate seas there are generally two 'blooms' of plankton, one in spring or early summer, the other in autumn; °phytoplankton; °plankton 'bloom'; °zoo plankton; °ill. 47 and 48.

plankton 'bloom' A time when plankton is at its most prolific; °plankton.

plastics Synthetic materials which replace natural and mineral materials to a degree. They are generally resistant to decay and/or corrosion.

plexiglass °Perspex.

plot Boating term: the way a course is laid off on a chart to allow for tide and possible °leeway.

pneumothorax Collapse of a lung due to entry of air into the pleural cavity. In diving, it is one of the results of a burst lung. Symptoms: pain in chest; cough; and possibly nose bleed.

poison Any substance which interferes with the chemistry (metabolism) of the body. Organic poisons are called toxins. The diver is more concerned with poisoning by gases, e.g. °carbon dioxide poisoning; °oxygen poisoning, etc.

Poland Polskie Towarzystwo Turystyczno Krajoznawcze, Warszawa 1, ul. Senatorska 11, Poland. Founded 1955.

polypropylene Inexpensive rope. It

floats, has high strength and absorbs little water, but kinks easily.

polythene Inexpensive rope. Slightly heavier than polypropylene. Absorbs no water. Hairy.

pooped A boat which has been boarded or even swamped by a wave from astern.

port Boating term: the left-hand side of a vessel when facing the bow with your back to the stern.

Portugal Federacao Portuguesa de Actividades Submarinas, Rua do Arco do Cego 90, 5°, Lisboa, Portugal. Founded 1954 as the Club Portugues de Casa Submarina.

pot Recompression chamber.

Pre Continent 1 Possibly the first underwater habitat experiment in saturation diving. Two men remained at 33 ft (10 m) for 7 days between 14 and 21 September 1962 at Marseilles. At this depth decompression was not necessary. Subsequent experiments have increased the depth and decompression is required; °saturation diving.

pregnancy Diving while pregnant seems to present few risks (a child of one of the authors had 18 dives before birth, and is a perfectly normal, healthy girl approaching her teens now). However, caution should be taken to avoid over-exertion, °nitrogen narcosis, and deep and/or prolonged dives near the °no-stop decompression times. Despite the above, it must be pointed out that very little work has been done on the effects of diving on pregnancy.

preservation The procedure of preventing deterioration. Metals should be kept dry, greased, painted, or plated. Organic material, in general, can be kept in a 70% ethyl alcohol or 5% formaldehyde solution. Wood can be preserved by soaking thoroughly to remove any salt, then inpregnating with polythylene glycol 4000 over a long period of time before drying out. Bronze may be cleaned in 3% benzo-tri-azol under gentle vacuum. Wrought iron is improved by immersion in a 5% solution of sodium sesquicarbonate. Pottery responds to a 10% solution of calgon for a long time, although local treatment with hydrochloric acid may be tried.

pressure Force per unit area. It can be expressed as: °bars; °atmospheres; mm/Hg; lbs/sq ins (p.s.i.); kg/sq cm; °Newtons/sq cm; etc.

pressure, absolute The total pressure,

49. Pressure: comparison of absolute and gauge

ABSOLUTE		GAUGE
1 atmosphere (ata) 1 bar 14·7 psi		zero

WATER SURFACE

ABSOLUTE		GAUGE
2 bar – 2 ata	10 metres	1 bar – 1 at
29·4 psi	33 feet	14·7 psi
3 bar – 3 ata	20 metres	2 bar – 2 ats
44·1 psi	66 feet	29·4 psi
4 bar – 4 ata	30 metres	3 bar – 3 ats
58·8 psi	99 feet	44·1 psi
5 bar – 5 ata	40 metres	4 bar – 4 ats
73·5 psi	132 feet	58·8 psi

including atmospheric, acting on an object. Thus the absolute pressure at a depth of 33 ft (10 m) is: 2 ata; 2 bars; 29·4 psi, etc.; °ill. 49.

pressure, ambient The surrounding pressure. At a depth of 33 ft (10 m) a diver would be at an ambient pressure of 2 ata or 1 atmosphere gauge.

pressure, atmospheric °Atmosphere; °atmospheric pressure.

pressure, effects of Solids and liquids are little affected by any pressure met in diving (the body tissues are reduced in volume by 1/20,000 for each atmosphere additional pressure). Gases and gas-filled spaces are however subjected to volume change. Increases in density and viscosity also occur with pressure; °barotrauma; °gas laws.

pressure gauge A mechanical device for indicating pressure. The common mechanism is based on a Bourdon tube, a curved metal tube, which pressure tends to straighten. Also, °depth gauge.

pressure, gauge Underwater pressure, taking atmospheric pressure as zero. Gauge pressure at a depth of 33 ft (10 m) is: 1 at; 1 bar; 14·7 psi, etc.; °ill. 49.

pressure, partial °Partial pressure.

pressure relief valve A spring-loaded valve designed to lift at a pre-set pressure. It is found in air compressor and regulator stages, where an up-stream valve is used. By lifting at the pre-set pressure, damage to the other mechanism, by over-pressurization, is prevented.

protective clothing A general term for suits worn by divers; °constant volume suit; °dry suit; °wet suit.

proton magnetometer A detector of ferrous metal. It can detect changes in the spin of protons in samples of distilled water. These changes in spin are caused by external magnetic fields such as wrecks. Sensitivities range from finding 2 gm at 50 m to 2,100 tonnes at 100 m. Greater sensitivities are possible, but not in portable instruments.

p.s.i. (psi) Abbreviation for pounds per square inch.

P.T.F.E. Poly tetra fluor ethylene. A plastic with non-stick properties. P.T.F.E. tape is used in gas-sealing mechanical threads, e.g. in sealing H.P. pipe unions and for sealing taper-thread pillar valves into their cylinders.

pulley A simple machine utilizing leverage in the form of blocks or pulleys to make work easier.

pulmonary barotrauma °Embolism; °emphysema; °pneumothorax.

pulse A shockwave in the blood of an artery synchronized with the beat of the heart and caused by the heart pumping blood round the body. The pulse is usually taken in the wrist (radial) or throat (carotid) and averages 60-80 beats per minute at rest.

purge button Button on the front or mouthpiece (second) stage of a regulator. When depressed, it causes a free flow of air, 'purging' water from the mouthpiece.

purge valve A valve through which water in a face mask can be blown or purged.

Q

Quaglia, Commendatore Giovanni Italian head of the Sorima Salvage Company of Genoa during the raising of the *Egypt's* gold, etc. in the 1920s–30s. The story is related in David Scott's *Seventy Fathoms Deep*.

quick-release A special release which enables weight-belts and/or scuba harnesses to be jettisoned immediately, simply, safely, and by the use of one hand only. Any system that does not fulfil all the above criteria should not be called a quick-release; °ill. 50.

Quilici, Folco Italian underwater pioneer. Author of *The Blue Continent* (1954).

50. Quick-release – just one of many different types
(N.B. This is not an ordinary buckle)

R

radar Now a common name, this derived from an abbreviation of Radio Detection and Ranging. The detection and location of distant objects by 'bouncing' radio waves off them.

rapture of the deep(s) Synonym for °nitrogen narcosis.

rash A blotchy, marbled rash covering large areas of the trunk is one sign of mild decompression sickness. It may or may not precede more severe symptoms.

rate The speed of a tide-stream.

rate of ascent Excess nitrogen leaves the blood during the ascent of a scuba diver. To control the rate of nitrogen loss and prevent decompression sickness, a steady ascent should be adhered to. Recommended rates are: U.S.N./R.N., 18 m (60 ft) per minute; R.N.P.L., 15 m (50 ft) per minute.

Rebikoff, Dmitri Parisian designer and builder of underwater lighting units for photography from the 1950s. Worked initially with °Broussard.

rebreathing The act of breathing the same air more than once. Rebreathing scuba uses a cylinder of pure oxygen. This oxygen is bled into a bag from which the diver inhales. He then exhales into the back via a filter that removes the carbon dioxide. This system is favoured by military forces because it eliminates exhaust bubbles, enabling the diver to go visually undetected, and by commercial divers because a relatively small cylinder can be used for a dive of long duration. Because this system has many attendant dangers, it is frowned upon by most amateur diving organizations; °carbon dioxide poisoning; °hypoxia, dilution; °oxygen poisoning.

recharging The act of re-filling a high-pressure cylinder. Care should be taken to avoid overheating the cylinder while it is being charged (air temperature rises when it is compressed), because this reduces the actual mass of air transferred and increases the risk of condensation inside the cylinder.

recompression The act of re-pressurizing a diver, usually in a compression chamber. This is generally a preliminary to therapeutic decompression.

recovery position °Coma position.

reducer A small orifice or valve used to reduce either volume flow or pressure of air. For example, a volume reducer may be used in a cylinder reserve valve (R-reserve) or in a high-pressure hose leading to a pressure gauge. This reduces air loss if the hose should rupture; °restrictor.

reel A device for carrying a line (rope) or hose neatly coiled up in such a way that it can easily be paid out and recovered.

refraction Light travels in straight lines

except when it crosses from a medium of one °refractive index into a medium of another refractive index. This 'bending' of light is called refraction.

refractive index A mathematical ratio expressing the light 'bending' effect of a medium. This is given by Snell's Law, which states that

$$\text{refractive index} = \frac{\text{Sine } \hat{\imath}}{\text{Sine } \hat{r}}$$

The refractive index of water is 1·33, air is 1·00, and glass averages 1·50.

regulator Also called a demand valve. A valve which reduces the pressure of air from a cylinder to that of °ambient. It automatically varies the given pressure with depth. Air only flows during inhalation, i.e. 'on demand'; °breathing resistance; °initial suction pressure; °P-factor.

relaxed An essential attitude of mind for a diver.

release °Quick-release.

repeat dives °Multiple dives.

repetitive dives These carry decompression penalties; °multiple dives.

reserve Air kept in reserve for use at the end of a dive. Ascent should start immediately the reserve is put to use; °J-reserve; °K-valve; °R-reserve.

residual air The volume of air which always remains in the lungs despite the most forced expirations. The amount that *cannot* be exhaled; °lung volume.

resistance to breathing The increase in the effort required to inspire/expire air due to any apparatus; °laminar flow; °turbulent.

respiration Technically, the process whereby energy is produced by the oxidation of food. In its commoner, wider sense, it is taken to include breathing, etc.

respiratory dead space °Dead air space.

respiratory rate The number of complete breaths taken in one minute. In an adult at rest this varies from about 8 to 16 breaths.

restoration °Preservation.

restrictor A device which narrows the bore of a pipe or orifice. This may be part of a reserve system; °reducer; °reserve.

resuscitation The act of restoring to life someone apparently dead, e.g. breathing or heart-beat ceased; °cardiac massage; °E.A.R.

retrosternal emphysema A form of °interstital emphysema located behind the sternum or breast bone.

reversed ear A form of °barotrauma where haemorrhage and/or rupture of the tympanum occurs due to excess pressure within the middle ear. It can occur on descent if the ears are covered, blocked or plugged. More rarely, it can occur on ascent.

Reynold's number This indicates the conditions under which a °laminar flow is converted into a °turbulent flow.

rip current A strong, narrow current moving away from the shore. It seems to be associated with troughs or depressions in the shoreline, or with narrow gaps in sand bars or reefs.

R.N.P.L. Royal Naval Physiological Laboratory.

R.N.P.L. Decompression Tables Possibly the safest decompression tables. First tested in 1966, published in 1972, and authorized for amateur use in 1975; °no-stop time.

rope Large cord. Most fibre ropes are 'right-handed', °hawser-laid. Rope was commonly sized by circumference, but sizing by diameter is becoming more common. Diameter in millimetres is 8 × circumference in inches; °cable-laid; °plaited.

rope signals These are used when a diver is roped to a surface tender. The signals are communicated by steady tugs or pulls. For amateurs, the signals should be simple and small in number. The set adopted by the B.S.A.C. is one of the most commonly used:

1 pull = Are you O.K.? *or* I am O.K.
2 pulls = Stop!
3 pulls = Go down *or*
I am going down.
4 pulls = Come up *or*
I am coming up.
5 pulls or more = Emergency.

rope strength The breaking loads or minimum breaking strains for ropes vary according to the size and type of rope, e.g. the breaking load for half-inch circumference sisal is 240 lbs (109 kg), while that of nylon of the same circumference is 700 lbs (318 kg). However, the breaking load only applies to new rope. Rope becomes progressively weaker with use. The strength of a rope is also reduced by splices (about 12%), when in water (10–15% for nylon), and by knots (15–50% depending on type of knot). Formulae for calculating breaking strains have been published, e.g. °manilla (7–144 mm) $2D^2/300$; nylon (4–96 mm) $5D^2/300$.

Rouquayrol, Benoit French mining engineer. With °Denayrouze, he invented the aerophore.

rowlock In boating, a space cut in the °gunwale, or metal or plastic crutches serving to hold the oars when rowing.

R-reserve Also known as an automatic reserve valve. In the scuba unit, the air flow is restricted to a permanent small orifice. When the air cylinder pressure falls to around 300 psi, insufficient air can pass at depth and the diver *must* ascend at once. Although this type of valve has its uses, it could be particularly dangerous in certain situations, e.g. cave diving; °depth compensated regulator.

rumbling The slow and prolonged rotation of a cylinder containing relatively large, sharp or abrasive objects. An efficient method of removing linings, scale or rust from inside an air cylinder without further weakening the wall.

Russia Federation for Underwater Sports of the USSR, B.P. 395, Moscow D-362, USSR. Founded 1959, although some clubs originated in 1950.

rust A brown oxide that readily flakes off and occurs on ferrous metals when exposed to a certain degree of moisture. Over 40% humidity is required for rusting to occur at normal temperatures. Apart from causing mechanical defects, rust is dangerous because it can remove metal from the walls of air cylinders, making them dangerously weak; °corrosion.

S

sacrificial anode Where corrosion in sea water is possible, a special anode of, say, zinc or aluminium is provided. In this way the anode is corroded, and the main body of metal is not. A sacrificial anode is fitted to many outboard motors.

safety catch A device for preventing the firing of a speargun.

safety fuse A slow-burning fuse for use with explosives. 1 ft (300 mm) takes about 30 seconds to burn; °cord-tex.

safety glass A glass which has been treated to reduce the possibility of injury in the event of its breaking. Two main types are used for face masks: **1.** Laminated, which is a sandwich of special plastic bonded between two layers of glass. It is rather heavy, and if it should break and splinter, the pieces will be jagged, but mostly the broken glass adheres to the plastic. **2.** Toughened or heat-treated, which has been heated and cooled rapidly from 650°C. This 'case-hardens' the glass and, in the event of it breaking, shatters into small pieces which, while quite sharp, are not as dangerous as the long slivers produced by ordinary glass. Sometimes plastic materials are incorrectly called safety glass.

safety line °Lifeline.

salinity The 'saltiness' of the sea. This varies from 2·9% of °salt in the polar seas to 3·55% in the tropics. It averages 3·33%. In the Dead Sea, salinity varies from 19·5% at the surface to 26·66% below 250 ft (76 m).

salt Commonly sodium chloride. A 'salt' has a wider meaning, being produced by the action of any base on any acid.

salvage This word covers a vast range of activities and situations from taking on tow an abandoned ocean liner to the recovery of some minor artifact from the sea bed. Note that everything found on or in the sea belongs to someone and the mere act of finding same will not make you the owner, although you may be able to keep it or a proportion of the monies if it is sold, depending on the specific laws of the country. A wreck or a ship residing outside territorial waters will invariably belong to the original owner according to the laws of most countries. However, every country has different laws relating to salvage.

Sampson post A strong post usually located in the forward half of a boat. Used for a variety of securing and holding purposes.

sand-blasting An abrasive cleaning process using sand or synthetic abrasives in an air or water current. It is a rapid and very efficient way of removing surface deposits such as rust. Because of its powerful scouring ability, this method should never be used in or on air cylinders, because some of the metal is invariably removed, weakening the walls.

saturation diving Diving for such prolonged periods that at a given depth the tissues are totally saturated with dissolved nitrogen (or other diluent). When this stage has been reached, decompression time is at a maximum and does not increase with prolonged exposure.

scattering The way in which rays of light are reflected by particles suspended in water, and scattered at all angles from their original path. A similar effect can distort the reading of an echo sounder; sometimes a shoal of fish will come between the echo sounder and the sea bed, forming a layer that 'scatters' the readings.

Schenck, Hilbert, Jr American. Joint author with °Kendall of *Underwater Photography*.

scombroid poisoning Under most circumstances the eating of scombroid fishes (mackerel, tuna, etc.) is without danger, but the flesh *can* become poisonous after exposure to the sun for two hours or more.

scooter A mechanically propelled device used to carry a diver at speed under water. It usually takes the form or shape of a 'torpedo', on which the diver hangs or rides. It is generally powered by batteries.

Scotland Scottish Sub-Aqua Club, 16 Royal Crescent, Glasgow G3 7SL, Great Britain. Founded 1953.

screw Boating term: an alternative name for a propellor.

Scripps Institute of Oceanography La Jolla, California. A branch of the University of California, Scripps is probably the best known and most respected oceanographic establishment in the world.

51. Scuba pack

scrub To remove a gas from circulation. Oxygen rebreathing scuba is a good example. Exhaled gas passes through a soda-lime filter, which 'scrubs' or removes the carbon dioxide.

scuba Self-contained underwater breathing apparatus. The common American name for aqualung. Although it could technically be used for any form of independent breathing apparatus such as oxygen rebreathing, it usually means diving on compressed air, independent of surface hoses or supplies; °scuba pack; °ill. 51, 52 and 53.

scuba pack A scuba or aqualung unit that also includes weights and a lifejacket of the °A.B.L.J. type, usually all housed in a plastic/fibreglass case; °ill. 51 and 52.

52. Scuba pack inside

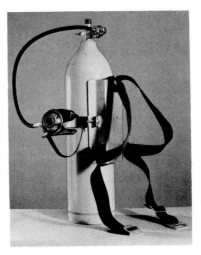

53. Scuba cylinder, harness (back pack) and single-hose regulator

sea The immediate effect of wind (it is a good/bad sea). The effect can be gauged from the height of the waves, according to the °international sea scale, which reads:

0	Calm	0 ft (0 m)
1	Smooth	0–½ ft (0–150 mm)
2	Light	½–2 ft (150–600 mm)
3	Moderate	2–5 ft (600 mm–1·5 m)
4	Rough	5–9 ft (1·5–2·7 m)
5	Very rough	9–15 ft (2·7–4·5 m)
6	High	15–24 ft (4·5–7·3 m)
7	Very high	24–36 ft (7·3–11 m)
8	Precipitous	36 ft plus (11 m plus)

seafire An oxy-hydrogen flame used in cutting metal under water.

seamanship Common sense and safety at sea. The ability to handle a boat well.

search Any means of locating lost objects under water. Common search patterns are: circular sweep; jackstay; rectangular; and swimline.

seasickness The exact cause of seasickness is unknown, but the probability of becoming afflicted is increased by: sitting in a heaving boat; cold; apprehension; unpleasant fumes such as exhaust smells; the sight of another person being sick; the after-effects of alcohol. Treatment consists of returning the affected person to shore as soon as possible. Drinks of cool water will help, even if soon brought up again. Incidentally, seasickness tablets are useless by the time the symptoms appear. The tablets also tend to make the taker drowsy – so could be dangerous for a diver.

sea state The condition of the sea in terms of wave height and wind velocity; °Beaufort wind scale; °sea (international sea scale); °swell.

sea water, composition of *Salts* (percentage of): sodium chloride 77·82; magnesium chloride 9·44; magnesium sulphate 6·57; calcium sulphate 3·44; potassium chloride 2·11; magnesium bromide 0·22. *Other elements* (in parts per million): chlorine 18980; sodium 10561; magnesium 1272; sulphur 884; calcium 400; potassium 380; bromine 65; carbon 28; strontium 13; boron 4·6; silicon 0–4·0; fluorine 1·4; nitrogen 0–0·7; aluminium 0·5; rubidium 0·2; lithium 0·1; phosphorus 0–01; barium 0·05; iodine 0·05; (Parts per thousand million): arsenic 10–20; iron 0–20; manganese 0·10; copper 0–10; zinc 5; lead 4; selenium 4; caesium 2; uranium 1·5; molybdenum 0·5; thorium 0·5; cerium 0·4; silver 0·3; vanadium 0·3; lanthanum 0·3; yttrium 0·3; nickel 0·1; scandium 0·04; gold 0·006; radium 0·0000002.

seaweed Any plant growing in the sea could be called a seaweed, but scientifically the term is reserved for green, brown and red algae only.

Secchi disc A device for assessing visibility under water. A disc, about 6 in (150 mm) in diameter and painted white, is lowered into the water via a cord through the center. Visibility is read off at the point the white disc vanishes. It was first used in 1865, and it does not seem to matter if the diameter is not within the measurements mentioned, as long as the same diameter is used all the time. Some workers have found that painting black and white quadrants on the disc makes the judgement of distance easier; °visibility.

second stage Where the pressure reduction by a regulator is done in two steps, the second step, usually from about 120 p.s.i. to ambient pressure, is called the second stage. In a °single-hose regulator, this is the mouth-held stage; °ill. 54.

semi-diurnal Twice a day. Tides experienced in Western Europe, including Britain, and other places. There are two high-water and two low-water tides each day.

set The direction of a tide-stream.

sextant A precise instrument used in navigation for measuring the angular distance of objects by means of reflection. Measuring the altitude of the

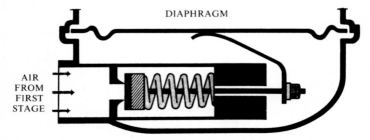

DIAPHRAGM

AIR FROM FIRST STAGE

54. Second stage: 'mouthpiece' stage of a single-hose regulator *(U.S. Divers)*

55. Sextant

sun helps to determine latitude. For divers, the sextant is mostly used to measure horizontal angles for position fixing; °ill. 55.

shallow water blackout Another name for oxygen syncope. It usually occurs with oxygen breathing aparatus. Appears to result from the combination of a number of factors, including breathing pure oxygen, hyperventilation, and suddenly increased intrapulmonary pressure; °syncope.

shallow water effect This occurs when a semi-diurnal tide pattern is distorted, so that there may be double high waters, double low waters, or a 'stand' at high water or low water.

sharing The act of two or more divers taking turns to breathe under water from one scuba unit. A lifesaving technique sometimes included in diver training schedules in case of air or equipment failure during a dive.

shark billy A pointed stick with which to fend off sharks. The point is more to prevent the end slipping off the shark's skin than to cause injury.

shock This is not the same as 'fright.' It is a state of collapse of the circulatory system, which can be fatal. It follows severe bleeding, extensive burns, bone fractures, excessive seasickness, severe decompression sickness – particularly after recompression – and other causes. Symptoms: the patient breaks out in a cold sweat, is very pale, and has a shallow, rapid breathing rate. There may also be a gasping for air, a rapid, weakening pulse, and he may be worried and confused. Unconsciousness and death are the ultimate symptoms. Treatment: reassure patient, lie him/her down (coma position, if unconscious) and prevent chilling. Remove to hospital, or at least call a doctor, as soon as possible.

shock wave A rapidly travelling explosion-induced phenomenon.

shore diving Diving from and returning to the shore. Boats are not involved. Depths are usually less than those obtained from a boat. Visibility, because of suspended coastal sediments, is often poor. Breaking waves and surf are additional hazards.

shortie Wet suit covering only the torso, upper arm and perhaps the head. For waters that are cool but not too cold.

shot-blasting Firing numerous pellets of lead shot at a metal surface to dislodge paint, rust, etc., without damaging the underlying metal.

shot line A line to which a very heavy weight (or 'shot') is fixed. It is used to guide the descent and ascent of divers. It must not be used as an anchor, because shot lines should be hung vertically.

Siebe, Augustus German instrument maker and gunsmith who settled in England in 1816. In 1840 he developed what is probably the first closed dress for helmet divers, which revolutionized diving. Founder of Siebe, Gorman & Co.

sign A medical term: deviation from the normal displayed by a casualty and observed by another person, e.g. skin pallor. An important diagnostic aid; °symptom.

signals In diving, various signals are used for communication. Hand

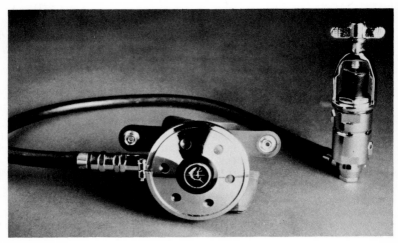

56. Single-hose regulator

signals are used for diver-to-diver communication under water; and for diver/surface cover. Rope signals are used for diver/tender messages. Light (torch) signals are used for communication when night diving. On a boat, if flags are flown, the °International Code is used. The one exception to the latter is the U.S.A., which uses a flag not in the International Code to indicate that divers are under water.

silica gel An adsorbent for water. It is sometimes coloured to show blue when new or dry, and pink when saturated. Will also adsorb oil vapour.

silicone A compound based on silicon rather than carbon. It can be produced as an oil, grease, resin or rubber. Characterized by its resistance to water and oxidation, including combustion. It is particularly stable at high temperatures.

Silvester-Brosch A manual method of resuscitation. Little used by divers – expired air resuscitation being preferred.

Singapore Underwater Federation of Singapore, Chinese YMCA, Palmer Road, Singapore 2. Founded 1969.

single-hose regulator A regulator with only one small-bore hose from the cylinder valve to the mouthpiece. Exhaust air is exhaled through ports in the mouthpiece. Generally a two-stage regulator: one stage attached to the pillar valve, the other located at the mouthpiece. Because of this, it is sometimes called a 'split stage'; °ill. 54 and 56.

single stage A regulator in which the reduction of pressure from cylinder to ambient pressure occurs in one step

or stage; °two stage.

sinus The sinuses are air-filled spaces in the frontal, sphenoid, ethmoid and maxillary bones of the skull. They connect with the air cavities of the nose. If the tissue lining the sinus is swollen – the result of a cold perhaps – the diver will not be able to equalize pressure under water and pain will result, perhaps accompanied by bleeding. You should not dive with an infected sinus; °ill. 57.

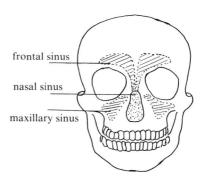

frontal sinus

nasal sinus

maxillary sinus

57. Location of sinuses in skull

sisal A cheap white fibre obtained from the leaves of the agave plant from Africa, Brazil, Indonesia and the West Indies. Sisal rope has only about three-quarters the strength of °manilla.

S.I. units The abbreviation stands for System International, an internationally recognized metric system of units; °metric system; °Newton.

skin-diver Technically an underwater swimmer without scuba, submerging solely on a lung full of air breathed on the surface and using only fins, mask and (optionally) snorkel. It is a mainly American term, the British name being 'snorkeller'. The term skin-diver is often, and incorrectly, used in the press to describe sports divers in general.

skin fold test A test for fatness or obesity. With the left arm hanging relaxed, the skin in the mid-triceps area should give a 'Harpenden caliper' reading below 15 mm.

slack water Technically a time when no tide is flowing. It usually occurs at the change-over point between ebb/flood, flood/ebb, although it can occur at other times depending on the shape of the coastline. Generally short-lived, it is often totally absent. Dives in tidal areas are often planned to coincide with slack water because at this time there is little or no current, and the period before and after has relatively weak currents. There is no specific rule to determine the time of slack water or even its exact geographical location, but any good nautical chart of the area will give details for slack water in that area.

slate Term used for an underwater writing surface. It is not made of slate, more often being of clear plastic, rubbed rough on one side (the writing side, with a lead pencil) and painted white on the other.

S.L.J. °Surface lifejacket.

slurp gun A large syringe-like device for collecting living creatures under water, whole and undamaged. It consists of a piston or plunger inside a large-diameter cylinder. A fish is approached, the cylinder placed near the fish, and the plunger pulled back quickly. This causes the fish to be sucked, unharmed, into the cylinder.

snorkel This enables a diver to breathe on the surface without the effort of raising his face from the water to breathe. It is not essential, but no diver should be without one. It could be a life-saver if the diver runs out of air and has to swim a long way back to shore or boat. A snorkel should have a tube length of between 12 and 14 inches (30–35 cm), and a diameter between $\frac{9}{16}$ and $\frac{7}{8}$ inch (15–20 mm). The actual measurements have been worked out in metric measurements, the other measurements are rough equivalents; °ill. 58.

snorkeller °Skin diver.

soda lime A mixture of calcium hydroxide and sodium hydroxide, obtained by slaking quicklime with caustic soda. It is supplied as dry granules. It is very efficient as an adsorbent of acid gases and is used in oxygen rebreathing units to absorb carbon dioxide.

soda lime cocktail A name given by divers to the caustic soda fluid resulting from the (accidental) action of water on soda lime. Highly dangerous and one of the worst kinds of corrosive poisons. This is just one of the reasons why oxygen rebreathers are frowned on by most amateur diving organizations.

solubility The amount to which one substance (the solute) will dissolve in a solvent. This amount varies, e.g. nitrogen is 5 times more soluble in oil than in water; °Henry's Law.

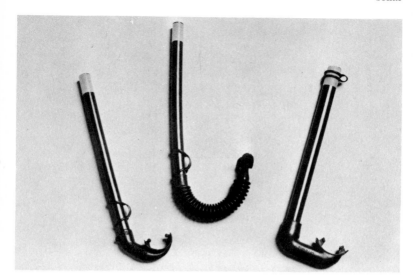

58. Various types of snorkels

sonar A means of detecting distance and direction of underwater objects using the reflections of sound pulses; °asdic.

sound The velocity of sound in air is 1,090 ft (332·2 m) per second; in water it travels at 4,440 ft (1,219·2 m) per second – around four times faster. Experiments have shown that high-pitch frequency sounds do not travel well under water – low-frequency low-pitch sounds travel far better. Foam neoprene hoods absorb sound very effectively under water, particularly at shallow depths before the material is compressed by the pressure. One effect of sound under water is that it does not appear directional to the diver. This means that, if a surfacing diver hears the propellor of a fast boat approaching, he will not know the direction it is coming from. In which case the best procedure, if possible, is to wait until the noise of the engine dies away.

sounding Measuring depth. This can be done with any instrument or apparatus, but the name derives from the time when depths were 'sounded' with a piece of lead on a length of rope.

South Africa South African Underwater Union, P.O. Box 201, Rondebosch, Cape Town, Republic of South Africa. Founded 1966.

space blanket A proprietary product consisting of a large sheet of aluminized plastic. It is claimed that it reduces heat loss and increases the chance of survival in exposed, hypo-

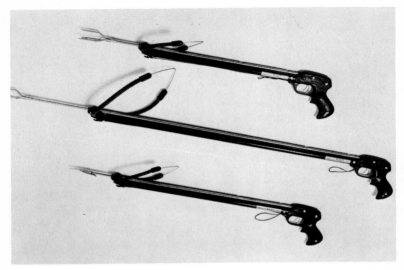

59. Spearguns: rubber powered

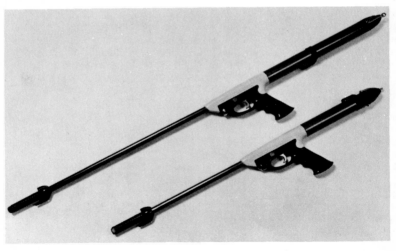

60. Spearguns: compressed air powered

thermic conditions; °hypothermia; °survival bag; °water chill; °wind chill.

Spain Federacion Espanola de Actividades Subacuaticas, Santolo 15, 3 la, Barcelona 6, Spain. The Spanish Federation organised the first World Congress of Underwater Activities in Barcelona in 1960. Founded in 1947 as the Committee for Underwater Activities.

spasm of the glottis Name given to the gasping and choking that occurs with a sudden influx of water during inspiration. The glottis closes and no air can enter the lungs. This is followed by painful gasping for air and panic. The latter often leads to drowning in the case of °'steam' swimmers.

spear Pointed, often barbed, projectile designed for catching fish. Spears should never be used to catch shellfish – mollusc or crustacean – of any kind.

spearfishing Hunting fish using a hand-powered spear or a speargun. In competitive spearfishing, the diver must not use scuba in any form and there are limits to the size and variety of fish that may be caught.

speargun Device for propelling a spear under water. The propelling power may be by hand, rubber strands, metal springs or compressed gas. Spearguns must never be loaded, fired, or even carried loaded out of the water; °ill. 59 and 60.

spear valve °Duck's beak valve.

specific gravity The density of a specific substance compared with that of pure water.

sphenoid sinus °Sinus.

spinal bend A serious form of °decompression sickness in which the lesion (bubble) is located in the spinal cord. Paralysis below the damage is usual, although it need not be permanent.

splice Method of joining two ropes, or finishing a rope end, or making a loop in a rope, by weaving the strands. Not applicable to plaited ropes.

spontaneous pneumothorax The sudden collapse of a lung when no apparent cause can be attributed. It has even been known to happen when the victim was walking along a street.

spring mooring A rope led diagonally from shore to a boat for mooring purposes.

spring tide A tide with the greatest range or rise and fall. Spring tides occur about every 14 days, just after new or full moon. Spring tides alternate with °neap tides.

squeeze The reduction in volume of a mask, hood or dry suit due to the compression of air contained within. In the case of a fold in a wet suit, it can squeeze or pinch the skin; °nips.

stage decompression Stopping for set times at set (pre-ordained) depths to allow for the gradual escape of excess nitrogen from the body; °decompression tables.

stage (decompression) Any one step of time/depth obtained from a °decompression table. The act of stopping at a particular depth for a specific time during decompression.

stage (regulator) A pressure reduction stop, usually in a regulator or compressor.

staggers A serious form of °decompression sickness. The victim is unable to maintain balance because of bubbles in the brain or inner ear.

stagnant hypoxia °Hypoxia, stagnant.

standard diver Another name for a °helmet or hard-hat diver.

standby diver A fully kitted up diver ready to enter the water at a moment's notice in the event of an emergency.

steam swimming Term used for 'ordinary' swimmers using no aids whatsoever.

stem The actual bow of a ship.

stern The rear end of a boat.

stop Synonym for °stage (decompression).

storm Weather conditions with a wind force of 11 on the °Beaufort wind scale.

stress corrosion Usually occurs when uniform corrosion is low. Somewhat similar to pitting. It occurs in stress-induced cracks. Cold working and welding are processes especially susceptible to stress corrosion. High-pressure air cylinders are frequently and highly stressed.

strobe flash °Electronic flash; °ill. 26.

Sub-aqua bronze medallion Award of the Royal Life-Saving Society. Designed, in collaboration with the B.S.A.C., for people involved in scuba diving. The award is one of the requirements for the B.S.A.C. First Class Diver Certificate.

suit, dry °Constant volume suit; °dry suit.

suit, wet °Wet suit.

supplemental air °Expiratory reserve; °lung volume.

surface cover The safety party on the surface of the water looking after the divers. May consist of one or more snorkellers, or of a small boat following the divers' marker buoy or bubbles.

surface demand Air supplied to a diver direct from the surface, via a line. The diver uses a regulator that comprises the second stage only; °hookah.

surface dive A diver submerging. There are different methods: °duck dive, °jack-knife, etc.

surface lifejacket (S.L.J.) A lifejacket designed to hold a person afloat on the surface of the water, but which is of little use or value for underwater work.

surfacing The act of rising to, or breaking, surface. A time of danger for divers. Buddies should surface facing each other. Each checks the 180° he can see behind his buddy, for any possible hazards. Unless on a lifeline from the surface, a solo diver should spiral slowly while surfacing, checking the surface over a 360° arc. In poor visibility and/or when boats are known to be in the vicinity, the diver should break the surface with one arm extended vertically above.

survival bag A polythene or similar plastic bag approximately 7 ft × 3 ft (2 m × 1 m) in size. It is used to enclose someone in danger of exposure or a victim of exposure/hypothermia, and prevent further chilling, increasing prospects of survival. The body is enclosed from the neck down, the head remaining uncovered; °hypothermia; °space blanket; °water chill; °wind chill.

Sweden Svenska Sportdykarforbundet, Box 925, 10133 Stockholm, Sweden. Founded 1958.

sweep One complete 'leg' or circle of a particular underwater search pattern.

swell The state of the sea when it is

affected by wind occurring at some other place or time. Internationally recognized swell scales are as follows:

Swell	Height	Spacing
0	none	none
1	low	short
2	low	long
3	moderate	short
4	moderate	average
5	moderate	long
6	heavy	short
7	heavy	average
8	heavy	long
9	confused	—

swimline A method of underwater search where divers are strung out along a rope. One diver sets the line to be swum. He tows a buoy, allowing the surface party to record the area covered. Reference: 'How to Find' – B.S.A.C. Paper No. 2.

Switzerland Federazione Svizzera di Sports Subaquei, Casa postale 183, 1000 Lausanne, Switzerland. Founded 1957 as the Swiss Centre for Underwater Sports.

symptom Medical term: a deviation from the normal detected in himself by the patient. The patient must be conscious.

syncope A faint (unconsciousness). In divers, syncope is due to the simultaneous occurence of two or more of the following, if it is specifically a diving cause: hyperventilation; alcohol after-effects; breathing pure oxygen; fatigue; hunger (rare); emotional disturbance, anxiety, etc.; incubating a feverish illness; poor vaso-motor tone (susceptible persons commonly faint at the thought of an injection or the sight of blood); increased intra-pulmonary pressure (holding the breath during exertion). Syncope generally occurs when breathing pure oxygen at pressure – formerly called shallow water blackout. Treatment: lay patient down, loosen tight clothing, and raise legs above level of the head.

systole The contraction of heart muscle. Arterial blood pressure during systole is 120 mm to 140 mm of mercury; °blood pressure; °diastole.

T

table A chart of figures used, for example, for the determination of decompression times; °decompression tables.

Tailliez, Captain Philippe French underwater pioneer; contemporary and companion of °Cousteau and °Dumas. Author of *To Hidden Depths*.

take off The tides are said to be 'taking off' when their amplitude is reducing from spring tide to neap tide.

tank Synonym for aqualung or scuba cylinder.

tank capacity °Cylinder capacity.

tank pressure °Cylinder pressure.

tap **1.** The means of turning a manual valve on or off. Fitted at the top of a cylinder pillar valve. **2.** An underwater sound signal made by tapping two objects together, e.g. knife handle on cylinder, etc. **3.** Device for cutting female threads.

taper valve Cylinder valve with a tapered thread. A lead or P.T.F.E. seal is essential. The tightening °torque for such valves is: aluminium cylinders 70–100 lbs/ft (32–45 kg/30 cm); steel cylinders 170–200 lbs/ft (77–90 kg/30 cm).

Tartaglia, Niccolo Italian who designed two types of diving bell around 1550. There is no indication that either was ever built, and it is doubtful whether they would ever have worked; °ill. 61.

61. One of Tartaglia's unworkable designs

teeth Teeth can cause trouble in diving (°aerodon talgia). False teeth can also be a danger, if they are not a good secure fit. In at least one fatality the victim was found with dentures dislodged in the mouth.

temperature, core The temperature of the heart, lungs, brain, liver, kidneys, etc., the vital organs. A reduction in core temperature is a serious matter. Temperatures and symptoms are as follows (temperatures approx):

37°C (98·5°F)	– Normal
36°C (96·5°F)	– Rise in metabolism. Sensation of severe cold.
35°C (95°F)	– Metabolism starts to fall.
34°C (93·5°F)	– Pulse slows and weakens.
33°C (91°F)	– Amnesia. Shivering stops. Mental confusion and semi-consciousness.
30°C (85°F)	– Unconsciousness. Heartbeat and respiration irregular.
28°C (83°F)	– Heart and lungs cease to function, but recovery still possible.
25°C (77°F)	– Irreversible death.

temperature, gas Gases expand with an increase in temperature, but, if the volume is held constant, the pressure increases. This situation is common in cylinder charging. Calculations for the changes is pressure due to temperature changes in scuba cylinders are based on the equation:

$$P_2 = P_1 \frac{t_2}{t_1}$$

where P_1 = original pressure
P_2 = final pressure
t_1 = original temperature
t_2 = final temperature

temperature, sea The mean annual temperatures of the oceans vary from almost zero in the polar regions to as much as 30°C (85°F) in the Pacific and Indian Oceans. Certain land-locked areas such as the Persian Gulf have surface temperatures as high as 32·2°C (90°F).

tender A diving assistant who is located at the shore or inboard end of a life-line. Often called a surface tender. Can also assist diver to dress, un-dress, etc.

therapeutic decompression Medically devised decompression schedules, used after recompression for the treatment of °decompression sick-ness. This takes place in a recompres-sion chamber. At certain stages, the diver may be required to breathe pure oxygen.

thermic lance Burns iron in oxygen, consuming 1 ft (30 cm) of lance every five seconds. Will cut iron and steel, and will actually melt concrete and granite. Efficient, but expensive.

thermocline The temperature bound-ary, often quite sharp (it can be felt quite distinctly, even when wearing protective clothing), between warmer and colder water. This effect occurs quite often in stagnant or slow-moving freshwater quarries and lakes. It is also noticeable in the sea. There are both permanent and temporary thermoclines.

thermometer An instrument for measuring temperature. Dial ther-mometers, using bi-metalic strips, are usually used by divers for con-venience, but they are not generally as accurate as liquid-filled thermo-meters.

thief strand A coloured strand running through a rope to aid identification.

Throckmorton, Peter American ar-chaeologist. One of his more im-portant excavations was the Cape Gelidonya site off Turkey. Author of *The Lost Ships* (1964).

thunderflash An explosive firework. It is designed to detonate with a loud bang. Thunderflashes may be used under water (having been ignited in air) as diver-recall signals by the tender or surface cover.

thwart Boating term: across the boat, at right-angles to the keel.

tidal lift The use of the rise of the tide to lift an object that is under water, which is then towed ashore. The object is quickly tied to something buoyant – oil drum, boat, etc. – when the tide is at its lowest. The rising tide or water then lifts the buoyant drum or boat and with it, hopefully, the object. The lift may have to be repeated many times, moving in-shore, to bring the object near the surface.

tidal volume Nothing to do with the sea, this is the amount of air which is normally breathed in and out at rest; °lung volume.

tide The periodic rise and fall of the sea due to the attraction of the sun and the moon. Some areas are not affected and are thus tideless; °diurnal; °semi-diurnal; °tide-stream.

tide-stream Current caused by the movement of the tides. Tide-streams are greatly modified by shorelines and the sea bottom contours; °inset; °rip current; °shallow water effect.

tide-table Printed tables setting out the forecast times and heights of high and low water at specific coastal ports. These forecasts can be upset by rain, wind and barometric effects. For example, the world tidal flow runs

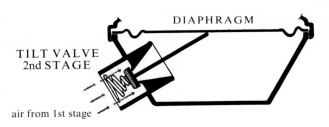

DIAPHRAGM

TILT VALVE
2nd STAGE

air from 1st stage

62. Tilt valve in mouthpiece of a single-hose regulator *(U.S. Divers)*

from west to east, so a steady easterly wind for a period could delay a tide, while a westerly wind would have the opposite effect.

tide-turn The time at which a tide-stream changes direction. This change need not be of 180°, nor need it necessarily occur at either slack water or between low or high water.

tilt valve A simple mechanical valve separating high-pressure air from low-pressure air. It is found in the second stage of some single-hose regulators; °ill. 62.

topmark A device on top of a navigation buoy, giving additional visual information about the buoy.

torque The turning effect; °taper valve.

tourniquet An outdated but still most effective method of stopping bleeding. The great danger of the method is that it causes further death of tissue. It consists of applying pressure between the wound and the heart, restricting or stopping circulation.

toxin An organic poison, i.e. a poison from a living or formerly living organism. The toxin of the tetanus bacillus is so powerful that one ounce of pure toxin could kill 30,000,000

tons of living matter.

T.P. Test pressure. The pressure to which a gas cylinder is filled during statutory pressure testing.

trachea The windpipe. Stretching from the glottis at the back of the tongue, it extends through the neck and upper chest to divide into the two bronchi.

transit Navigational term: a line joining two fixed objects (e.g. the white church spire in line with the factory chimney third from left). Used out at sea as a bearing. If suitable transits are available, this provides a very accurate position-fixing line.

transom A transverse vertical timber across the stern of a boat. This is the section to which an outboard motor is usually attached when in use.

travel sickness Nausea, vomiting and acute illness which affect many people while at sea or travelling in a vehicle. Not enough is known about the cause, but it is almost certain that it is related to, or is the same thing as, seasickness.

Trieste An Italian-built °bathyscaphe designed by Auguste °Piccard, a Swiss physicist. First descent in August 1953 to 3,500 feet off Naples, manned by Piccard and his son Jacques.

triple set A three-cylinder scuba unit.

trot A fisherman's line of crab or lobster pots, connected with rope into one unit. Thus, when the first one is pulled up, the others automatically follow.

true north The direction along the geographical meridian (line of longitude) from the observer towards the north pole. Not the same as °magnetic north.

turbid Reduced underwater visibility due to suspended sediment. A condition often encountered in lakes, rivers and coastal areas.

turbulent When a fluid moves at a velocity above a critical velocity, it becomes turbulent, i.e. the velocity at a fixed point fluctuates with time in an almost random way. Mass transfer is considerably greater than in a corresponding laminar flow. Flow rates > 40 litres air/minute in the human respiratory system are largely turbulent (Miles); °laminar; °Reynold's number.

Turkey Sualti Sporlari Federasyonu, Melek Han Kat 2, No 18, Karakoy-Istanbul, Turkey. Founded 1970.

twelfths rule An approximate method of determining the height of the tide by dividing the range into twelfths and the time by six. It applies to areas which have two high-water and two low-water tides every 24 hours. Calculations are as follows:

				Total differ-ence
1st hour	rise/fall	$= \frac{1}{12}$ of range		$\frac{1}{12}$
2nd ,,	,,	$= \frac{2}{12}$	,,	$\frac{3}{12}$
3rd ,,	,,	$= \frac{3}{12}$	,,	$\frac{6}{12}$
4th ,,	,,	$= \frac{3}{12}$	,,	$\frac{9}{12}$
5th ,,	,,	$= \frac{2}{12}$	,,	$\frac{11}{12}$
6th ,,	,,	$= \frac{1}{12}$	,,	$\frac{12}{12}$

twin hose A regulator in which the reduction stage(s) and exhaust valve are in one unit, which is attached to the cylinder °pillar valve when in use. This necessitates both an inlet hose and an exhaust hose to and from the mouth – the twin hoses. It has the advantage that exhaust bubbles are released behind the head, not around

63. Twin-hose regulator

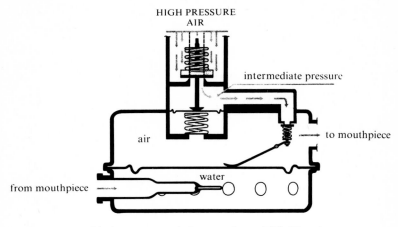

HIGH PRESSURE
AIR

intermediate pressure

air

to mouthpiece

from mouthpiece

water

64. A two-stage twin-hose regulator *(U.S. Divers)*

the mouth (as with a single hose) where the bubbles can obscure vision; °ill. 63 and 64.

twin-set A two-cylinder scuba or aqua-lung unit.

two stage A regulator in which the pressure reduction occurs in two steps or stages. Available in both twin-hose and single-hose models, although virtually all single-hose regulators are of two-stage construction nowadays; °ill. 64.

two-stroke Cycle of the internal combustion engine in which the crank-case compression is used to move petrol/oil mixture and exhaust gases. No valves are needed, and a power stroke alternates with the filling/scavenging stroke.

tympanum The ear-drum separating the outer and middle ear; °ear.

U

ultra-violet light Radiation from outside the earth's atmosphere. Responsible for sunburn and for perishing rubbers. The latter is the reason why diving equipment should not be left in sunlight.

unconsciousness Distressing enough on land, unconsciousness under water is invariably fatal. There are four degrees of consciousness: **1.** full–which

65. Undersuit giving extra warmth for cold water diving

is the normal state; **2.** drowsiness – when the victim can be aroused but only with difficulty; **3.** stupor – when the victim can only be aroused by painful stimulus; and **4.** coma – com-plete unconsciousness. Types 3 and 4 are dangerous states; °coma position.

undersuit Foam neoprene torso-fitting protective clothing. It fits under a wet suit jacket to add extra insulation for

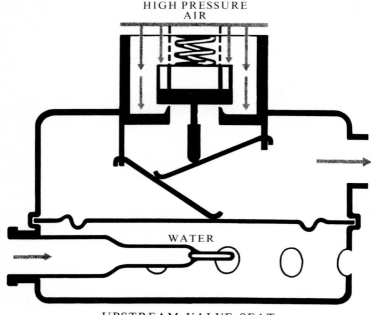

HIGH PRESSURE
AIR

WATER

UPSTREAM VALVE SEAT

66. Upstream valve in a single-stage twin-hose regulator *(U.S. Divers)*

extremely cold waters; °ill. 65.

uniform corrosion Shifting anodic/ cathodic areas cause more or less even corrosion, so that the metal becomes evenly thinner. In a way, the opposite to pitting and similar forms of corrosion.

United States of America Underwater Society of America, Ambler, Pennsylvania 19002, U.S.A. Founded 1959, although many clubs originated in the 1950s.

universal gas constant 0·082 l/at/mole/ °absolute.

upstream A valve mechanism which opens *against* the moving gas. Only a very light spring, if any, is used to hold it in the closed position. It becomes easier to open as the pressure falls; °balanced; °downstream; °ill. 66.

Uruguay Federacion Uruguaya de Pesca Amateur, Canelones 978, sede deportiva, Riachuelo 169, Montivideo, Uruguay. Founded 1973, although many of the clubs originated in the 1950s.

U.V. Abbreviation for ultra-violet light.

V

Valsalva manoeuvre Technical term for pressurizing the nose, lungs and, via the Eustachian tubes, the ears. Achieved by exhaling against a closed nose and mouth. Also called °ear clearing.

valve °Demand valve; °downstream; °J-reserve; °K-valve; °pressure relief valve; °regulator; °reserve; °R-reserve; °single-stage; °two stage; °upstream.

Van der Waal's equation A more correct representation of the behaviour of ordinary gases than the °gas equation:

$$(P + \frac{a}{V^2}) \ (V - b) = RT$$

P = pressure
a = constant depending on nature of gas
V = volume occupied by one gram-molecule of the gas
b = volume of the gas molecules
R = universal gas constant
T = absolute temperature

variation The difference in amount and direction between °magnetic north and °true north. This amount varies annually and geographically.

veer A change in wind direction in a clockwise manner.

vein A major blood vessel returning blood to the heart. Veins are nearer the skin than arteries, carry de-oxygenated blood (other than pulmonary veins) and carry the blood at low pressure. The blood is dark red.

Velcro A patent fastening consisting of minute plastic hooks on a sheet of similar material on the one hand, and which is pressed onto another sheet consisting of loops. It is easily opened and closed, but is very secure. It is found in place of a zip on some wet suits.

velocity ratio The ratio of the distance a force moves to the distance an object moves at the same time. Used for calculations involving pulleys; °mechanical advantage.

Venezuela Federacion Venezolana de Actividades Submarinas, Avenida Lasalle, entre la 1° y 2° Transversal, Quinta Nemrod, Sebucan, Caracas, Venezuela. Founded in 1955 as the Centro Submarinista de Caracas.

venting The act of removing air or allowing it to escape (*a*) from a dry suit, e.g. opening a wrist seal above water while the rest of the suited diver is below water, or (*b*) from an A.B.L.J. by actuating a vent valve or venting the mouthpiece.

venturi A narrow pipe section between two wider sections. There is a drop in pressure in the narrow section. This effect is used to improve breathing characteristics in some regulators by reducing the inspiratory effort.

vertigo A feeling of rotation or giddyness. Often happens when looking downwards from a height, hence it can affect a diver when looking over

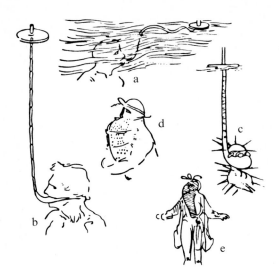

67. Some of da Vinci's drawings: (a, b) snorkels;
(c) snorkel attached to a helmet with windows; (d)
scuba with air reserve on diver's chest; (e) diver in
leather suit with sand-bags for ballast

a submarine cliff or shelf or over the side of a large wreck; °alternobaric vertigo.

vest Undergarment made of foam neoprene. Worn under a wet suit jacket for extra warmth. Similiar to, but not as warm or substantial as, an undersuit.

Vinci, Leonardo da Artist, scientist, genius (1452–1519). Da Vinci left many drawings pertaining to diving; free divers wearing hand paddles, submarines and snorkel-like apparatus. None of them were ever tested, and in any case most would not have worked; °ill. 67.

vis Abbreviation for visibility.

viscosity Gas viscosity is independent of density. Viscosity affects the °laminar flow.

visibility The subjective opinion of how far the eye can see under water. Visibility may vary from less than 1 in/2 cm in some rivers and harbours to 230 ft or 70 m in some oceans and clear lakes. On land, the meteorological definition of a 'dense fog' is visibility less than 140 ft or 50 m. It is rare to get underwater visibility this good and in some waters such as those surrounding Britain it is never, ever, as good as this; °Secchi disc.

vision Underwater vision is hampered by the laws of physics. The human eye has evolved to work in air, but when in water it becomes so short-sighted that it cannot form a sharp image at any distance. Contact lenses have been devised which permit perfect underwater vision, but it is more usual to enclose the eyes in a pocket of air with a glass/water demarcation for visibility – the face mask. However, because light travels at different speeds through air and water, distortion is produced by this combination. Refraction is the cause. This distortion causes objects seen under water to appear larger or nearer than they really are; in fact, $\frac{3}{4}$ of their true distance away and $\frac{1}{3}$ larger. Divers, however, soon adapt to this situation; °ill. 68.

visual aid An object or article used to attract the interest of an audience using sight, e.g. chart, film, slide, model. Invaluable for instructors and teachers.

vital capacity The maximum amount of air which can be moved into and out of the lungs by means of forced inspiration and expiration; °lung volume.

volume Usually measured in cubic feet, cubic yards, cubic metres, cubic centimetres, gallons or litres. Random equivalents are: 1 cu ft = 28 litres: or 6·24 gallons; 1 cubic metre = 35 cu ft.

vulcanize The treatment of natural rubber by heat and pressure, with the addition of sulphur. It changes the rubber, making it less thermoplastic, more elastic, stronger and more resilient. A method frequently used to repair tears or holes in rubber.

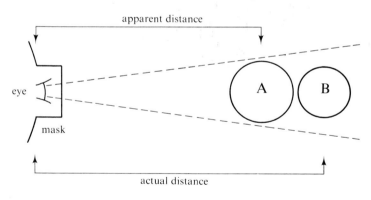

68. Vision

W

washer A ring-like device for making nuts more secure or for sealing some gap. Washers may be made of copper, leather, mild steel, neoprene, rubber, nylon, etc. It is probably most familiar to divers as a nylon or neoprene washer for a pillar valve/regulator connecting point, although washers at this junction ᴌᴧve given way largely to °O-rings.

watch Underwater, a watch is essential for decompression, certain forms of navigation, or simply for recording the duration of the dive. No watch is totally waterproof at any depth, but a watch can be guaranteed not to leak down to certain depths. This depth should be indicated on the face and is usually expressed in atmospheres, feet or metres. The best watches are pressure-tested down to at least 660 ft, 200 m or 20 ats. However, there are many superb diving watches that have a shallower limit than this. A diving watch must have a rotating bezel for recording elapsed time. Where helium is used in the breathing mixture, still greater precautions have to be taken in pressure proofing and some watches incorporate what is known as a helium valve.

water A compound of hydrogen and oxygen with the empirical formula H_2O. Specific gravity 1. Density 1 qm/cc or 62·4 lbs/cu ft. Freezing point 0°C (32°F). These figures refer to distilled water, however, not ordinary °sea water, which has many other chemicals including salt in it – this affects density, etc. For example, salt water is heavier than fresh water and freezes at a lower temperature; °salinity.

water capacity (W.C.) The weight or volume of water which a cylinder can hold. This is obtained by weighing during manufacture. By a simple calculation, the volume of air in a cylinder at any pressure can be deduced:

W.C. 20 lb

$$\text{empty volume at 11 ats} = \frac{20}{62\cdot5}\,\text{cu.ft}$$
$$= 0\cdot32\,\text{cu.ft}$$

full volume at 200 ats = 200 × 0·32 cu.ft
= 64 cu.ft

or

W.C. 14 litres
empty volume at 1 at = 14 litres
full volume at 200 ats = 200 × 14
= 2,800 litres

water chill The thermal conductivity of water is 240 times greater than still air. Heat is, therefore, conducted from the skin very rapidly when in contact with water, causing water chill; °evaporation; °wind chill.

wave Waves are created by the wind. The stronger the wind, the larger and longer the waves. Wave effects lessen with depth; °fetch; °sea; °swell.

way Nautical terms: **1.** Give way – allow another vessel right of way. **2.** Under way – a moving vessel. **3.** Way (weigh) anchor – to raise the anchor from the bottom and bring it inboard.

weather The behaviour of wind, rain, snow, etc. To some extent forecasts can be made, but even the most scientific are far from perfect. However, short-range forecasting – say for the next several hours – can be very accurate indeed and divers should make the most of this. Before a boat dive out at sea, the meteorological office should be consulted.

wet suit An insulating diving suit.

Protective clothing. A thin film of water is allowed to enter the suit. This film is trapped next to the skin and is warmed up by the body. The close fit of the suit prevents the water circulating and the cellular construction of the material – commonly foam neoprene from 3–6 mm thick – prevents or reduces heat loss. The suit material may, in addition, be lined with stockinette or towelling for comfort and extra strength. The suit seams may be sealed with a neoprene contact adhesive or be stitched. If the latter, it is essential that the material is lined. Wet suits can be home-made (partly prepared kits are a popular form), are easily repaired and can be

69. For economy you can purchase a wet suit kit ready marked out, which only needs cutting and glueing

70. Wet suit

71. Wet suit gloves

relatively inexpensive. They do not suffer from °nips or °squeeze, and tears or holes do not cause a disastrous loss of buoyancy, as they do in a dry suit; °ill. 69, 70, 71.

whipping The binding at the end of a rope to prevent it fraying.

wind The movement of air over the surface of the earth. Wind affects the surface of the sea; °Beaufort wind scale; °sea; °swell.

wind chill The cooling effect of moving air – not the evaporation cooling of wet skin or clothing.

work Work is done when a force produces a motion. The °S.I. unit of work is the joule (J) – 1 Newton moving 1 m is a joule.

work-harden Changes in the structure and behaviour of metals as they are worked beaten or flexed. For example, copper becomes less ductile and less flexible as it is worked; it can be restored to its former state by annealing.

working pressure (W.P.) The maximum pressure to which a gas cylinder should be charged for use. Many

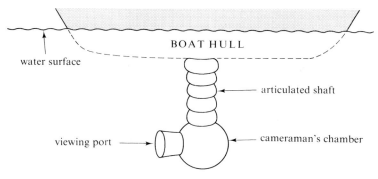

BOAT HULL

water surface

articulated shaft

viewing port

cameraman's chamber

72. The Williamson tube

compresser operators overcharge cylinders by 10%, on the assumption that the air is warm and the pressure will reduce as the contents cool. This procedure is not to be recommended; °fatigue.

Williamson, John Ernest The first underwater cine photographer (1914). His Williamson tube was a shaft underneath a boat, which gave access to an observation chamber, through which Williamson first photographed the underwater world of Chesapeake Bay. It was really his father's design, but with it Williamson achieved fame and fortune. Author of *Twenty Years Under the Sea*; °ill. 72.

wreck Any vessel, part of a vessel, cargo, fittings, or anything which may be found on or near the coast. To the average diver, however, a wreck is a vessel or the remains of one lying on the sea bed; °derelict; °flotsam; °jetsam; °ligan; °salvage.

X

xenon A noble or inert gas. The most highly narcotic of the noble gases. It has been used as a surgical anaesthetic.

X-ray Name given to a photograph taken by irradiation by X-rays. Taken as a routine examination for lung lesions, which could be a danger to the diver.

Y

yaw Sideways movement of a vessel so as to point the bow in a new direction. Can be caused by heavy waves.

Yugoslavia Savez za Sportski Ribolev na Moru i podvodne Aktivnosti SFRJ, Rijeka, U1. Matije Gupca 2, Yugoslavia. Founded 1953.

Z

zip Also called a zipper or zip fastener. A device for rapidly closing and opening apertures in clothing. Nylon zips have proved invaluable for wet suits. Waterproof zips are made for dry suits. The teeth are made from a nickel alloy and are held on to the coated fabric by U-shaped brass clamps in such a way that the material is not cut or pierced in any way.

zoo plankton Animal °plankton. It generally feeds on the °phytoplankton.

BIBLIOGRAPHY

Admiralty Diving Manual (HMSO, 1972)
Aldridge, Undersea Hunting for Inexperienced Englishmen (Allen & Unwin)
Allen, B., Skin Diving and Snorkeling (J. B. Lippincoft, 1973)
Allen, E. J., Science of the Sea (Challenger Society, 1928)
Alpers, A., Dolphins (Houghton Mifflin, Boston, 1960)
Atkinson, J., Skin Diving (Foulsham, 1962)

Barada, B., Skin Diving Annual (*Skin Diver* magazine)
Barrett & Yonge, Pocket Guide to the Seashore (Collins, 1960)
Bartlett, N., The Pearl Seekers (Arrow, 1954)
Barton, R., Oceanology Today (Aldus, 1970)
Bass, G. F., Archaeology Under Water (Thames & Hudson, 1966)
     A History of Seafaring (Thames & Hudson, 1972)
Beach, E. L., Submarine! (Holt, Reinhart & Winston, 1953)
Beebe, W., Half Mile Down (Harcourt Brace, New York, 1934)
Beebe, W., Book of Bays (Bodley Head, 1947)
Behenna, J., Westcountry Shipwrecks (David & Charles, 1974)
Bellamy, D., The Life-giving Sea (Hamish Hamilton, 1975)
Bennett & Elliott, The Physiology and Medicine of Diving and Compressed
     Air Work (Bailliere, Tindall & Cassell)
Berge, V., Pearl Diver (Heinemann, 1930)
Berman, B. D., Encyclopedia of American Shipwrecks (The Mariners Press,
     1972)
Blair, C., Diving For Treasure (Barker, 1961)
Borghese, V., The Sea Devils (Melrose, 1952)
Boswell, D., Loss List of Grimsby Vessels (Grimsby Public Library, 1969)
Brennan, M., Underwater Swimming (Arco, 1962)
Bridges, L., Mask and Flippers (W. H. Allen, 1961)
Briggs, P., 200,000,000 Years Beneath the Sea (Cassell, 1972)
Brightwell, L. R., Sea Shore Life of Britain (Batsford, 1947)
Brookes, G., Underwater Swimming (Educational Products)
Brown, T. W., Sharks – The Search for a Repellent (Angus & Robertson,
     1973)
Bruce, H. J., Twenty Years Under The Sea (Stanley Paul, 1939)
Brunetal, The Galathea Deep Sea Expedition (Allen & Unwin, 1956)
Burgess, R. F., Sinking, Salvages & Shipwrecks (American Heritage, 1970)

Burke, The Underwater Handbook (Muller)
Butterfield, A., The Coral Reef (Hamlyn)

Carrier, R. and B., Dive (Kaye & Ward, 1963)
Carrington, A Biography of The Sea (Chatto & Windus, 1960)
Carson, R., The Edge of the Sea (Staples, 1955)
    The Sea Around Us (Staples, 1951)
Carter, C., Cornish Shipwrecks – The North Coast (David & Charles, 1970)
Casson, The Ancient Mariners (Gollancz, 1954)
Cayford, E., Underwater Work (Cornell Maritime Press, 1959)
Ciampi, E., Skin Diving
Clark, E., Lady With A Spear (Heinemann, 1954)
Clarke, A. C., Coast of Coral (Muller, 1954)
    The Challenge of The Sea (Holt, Rinehart & Winston, 1960)
    Treasure of the Great Reef (A. Barker, 1964)
    Indian Ocean Adventure (A. Barker, 1962)
Cleator, P. E., Underwater Archaeology (Hale, 1973)
Clegg, J., Freshwater Life of the British Isles (Warne, 1952)
    Pond and Stream Life (Blandford, 1963)
Codrington, Guide to Underwater Hunting (A. Coles, 1954)
Cohen, P., The Realm of the Sub (Collier-Macmillan)
Cohen, S., Red Sea Diver's Guide (Taracoda, 1975)
Coleman, J. S., The Sea and Its Mysteries (1950)
Condon, T., Beneath Southern Seas (Findiver, c. 1969)
Constance, A., The Impenetrable Sea (Oldbourne, 1958)
Cook, Exploring The Sea (Abelard-Schuman)
Copplestone, V. M., Shark Attack (Pacific, Melbourne, 1968)
Croft, J., Life in the Sea (Hamlyn, 1969)
Cousteau, J-Y., The Silent World (Hamilton, 1953)
    World Without Sun (Heinemann, 1965)
    The Shark (Cassell, 1970)
    Life and Death in a Coral Sea (Cassell, 1971)
    Diving for Sunken Treasure (Cassell, 1972)
    The Whale (Cassell, 1972)
    Act of Life (Angus & Robertson, 1972)
    Quest for Food (Angus & Robertson, 1973)
    Octopus and Squid (Cassell, 1973)
    Oasis in Space (Angus & Robertson, 1973)
    Galapagos, Titicaca, Blue Holes (Cassell, 1974)
    Sea Lion, Elephant Seal, Walrus (Cassell, 1974)
    Mammals in the Sea (Angus & Robertson, 1975)
    Man Re-enters the Sea (Angus & Robertson, 1975)
    A Sea of Legends (Angus & Robertson, 1975)

Provinces of the Sea (Angus & Robertson, 1975)
Pharoahs of the Sea (Angus & Robertson, 1975)
Instinct and Intellect (Angus & Robertson, 1975)
Dolphins (Cassell, 1975)
Critchley, G. R., Ship Salvage
Cowan, E., Oil and Water (Kimber)
Crile, J. and B., Treasure Diving Holidays (Collins, 1954)
Cropp, B., Shark Hunters (Macmillan, New York, 1971)
Cross, E. R., Underwater Photography and Television (Exposition Press, 1954)
Culpin, H., Underwater Exploration (Muller)

Daly, R. A., Floor of the Ocean (1942)
Darnell, Underwater Life of the British Isles (Ward Lock, 1960)
Davies, C. N., Design and Use of Respirators (B.O.H.S., 1962)
Davies, W., Skin Diving for Boys (Scout Association, 1959)
        Venture Underwater Swimming (Faber & Faber)
Davis, Sir R. H., Deep Diving and Submarine Operations (St Catherine's Press, 1962, 7th edition)
Deas & Lawler, Beneath Australian Seas (Reed)
Dickinson, C., British Seas (Eyre & Spottiswood, 1963)
Diole, P., The Seas of Sicily (Sidgwick & Jackson)
        The Underwater Adventure (Sidgwick & Jackson, 1953)
        4,000 Years Under the Sea (Sidgwick & Jackson, 1954)
        Underwater Exploration (Sidgwick & Jackson, 1954)
Diver Support Systems (Society for Underwater Technology, 1975)
Doak, W., The Elingamite (Hodder & Stoughton, 1969)
Dobbs, H., Camera Underwater (Focal Press, 1962)
        Underwater Swimming (Collins)
Douka, G., The World Beneath the Waves (Allen & Unwin, 1954)
Du Cross, Skin Diving in Australia (Angus & Robertson, 1960)
Dugan, J., Man Under the Sea (Harper Bros, New York, 1956)
        Undersea Explorer (1957)
Dumas, F., Deep-Water Archaeology (Routledge & Keegan Paul)
Dumbar, J., The Lost Land (Collins, 1958)
Dutton, H. F., Swimming Free (Heinemann, 1972)

Eales, Littoral Fauna of Great Britain (Cambridge University Press)
Edwards, Islands of Angry Giants (Hodder & Stoughton, 1969)
Eibl-Eibesfeldt, I., Land of a Thousand Atolls (McGibbon & Kee, 1965)
Ellsberg, E., On the Bottom (1929)
Engelhardt, W., Pond-Life (Burke, 1964)

Falcon-Barker, Roman Galley Beneath the Sea (Brockhampton Press)
      1600 Years under the Sea (Muller)
      Devil's Gold (1969)
Faulkner, D., The Hidden Sea (Viking Press, New York, 1970)
Foucher-Creteaux, J., My Adventures Under the Sea (Muller, 1957)
Frey and Tzimoulis, Camera Below (Association Press, New York)
Frost, H., Under the Mediterranean (Routledge & Keegan Paul)
Furneaux, W. S., Life in Pond and Stream (1960)

Gaskell, T. F., Under the Deep Oceans (Eyre & Spottiswood, 1960)
      The Gulf Stream (Cassell, 1972)
George, S. C., Jutland to Junkyard (Patrick Stephens, 1973)
Gibbings, R., Blue Angels and Whales (1947)
Gilbert, P. W., Sharks and Survival (Heath, Boston, 1963)
Gilly, W. O. S., Shipwrecks of the Royal Navy (Parker, 1857, 3rd edition)
Gilpatrick, G., The Complete Goggler (Kaye)
Glatt, Underwater Navigation (Sea-well Engineering, 1960)
Godfrey and Lassey, Shipwrecks of the Yorkshire Coast (Daleman, 1974)
Gorskey, Mediterranean Hunter (Souvenir, 1954)
      Moana (Elek, 1956)
Grace, V., Amphorae and the Ancient Wine Trade (American School of
      Classical Studies, Princeton, 1961)
Greenberg, J., Underwater Photography Simplified (Seahawk, 1956)
Greenberg, J. and I., The Living Reef (Seahawk, 1971)
Grosset, H., Down to the Ships in the Sea (Hutchinson, 1953)
Gruss, R., The Art of the Aqualung (MacGibbon)

Haas and Knorr, Marine Life (Burke, 1966)
Hadfield, R. L., Sea-Toll of Our Time (Witherby, 1930)
Haldane, J. S., and Priestly, J. G., Respiration (Clarendon Press)
Haldane, J. S., Life at High Pressures (Penguin)
Hampton, T., Master Diver and Underwater Sportsman (A. Coles, 1955)
Hardy, A. C., Wreck – SOS (Crosby Lockwood, 1944)
      Hardy, Sir A., The Open Sea (Collins, 1956)
Hartwig, G., The Sea (Longmans Green, 1973, 4th edition)
Hass, H., Under the Red Sea (Jarrold, 1952)
      Diving to Adventure (Jarrold, 1952)
      Men and Sharks (Jarrold, 1954)
      I Photographed Under the Seven Seas (Jarrold, 1956)
      We Came from the Sea (Jarrold, 1958)
      Expedition into the Unknown (Hutchinson, 1965)
      To Unplumbed Depths (Harrap, 1972)
      Conquest of the Underwater World (David & Charles, 1975)

Hass, L., Girl on the Ocean Floor (Harrap, 1972)
Hill, L. E., Caisson Sickness (Edward Arnold)
Hodgson, D., Dive! Dive! Dive! (Luscombe, 1975)
Houot and Willm, 2000 Fathoms Deep (Harrap, 1955)
Hussein, F., Living Underwater (Studio Vista, 1970)
Huxley, T. H., The Problem of the Deep Sea (essay, 1894)

Idyll, C. P., Abyss (Constable, 1964)
    Exploring the Ocean World (Crowell, New York, 1972)
Ivanovic, V., Modern Spearfishing (Kaye & Ward, 1974)

Jackman, Marine Aquaria (Cassell)
Jefferis and McDonald, The Wreck Hunters (Harrap)
Jenkins, J. T. Fishes of the British Isles (Warne, 1958)
John, D. H. O., Photography on Expeditions (Focal Press)
Johnstone, P., The Archaeology of Ships (Bodley Head, 1974)
Jones, I. W., Shipwrecks of North Wales (David & Charles, 1973)
Jones, M. L., Guide to Skin Diving and Underwater Spearfishing (Universal
    Sales, California, 1952)

Karneke, Navy Diver (Hale)
Keeble, P., Ordeal by Water (1957, 2nd edition)
Kenyon, L., Discovering the Undersea World (University of London Press,
    1961)
Kimmins, R. J., Underwater Sport on a Small Income (Hutchinson, 1956)
Kuenen, Marine Geology (J. Wiley, 1960)

Labat, P., Marvellous Kingdom (Odhams, 1956)
Lanfranco, G. G., Complete Guide to the Fishes of Malta (1960)
Larn and Carter, Cornish Shipwrecks: The North Coast (David & Charles,
    1969)
Larsen, E., Men Under the Sea (1955)
Latil, P., Underwater Naturalis (Jarrold, 1954)
Lilly, Mand and Dolphin (Gollancz, 1961)
Lines, B., Downunder (Hale, 1972)
Lomer, G., Diving Guide to the Bahamas (Argos, 1975)

Macan and Worthington, Life in Lakes and Rivers (1951)
Marsden, P., Wreck of the Amsterdam (Hutchinson, 1974)
Marshall, N. B., Aspects of Deep Sea Biology (1954)
Marx, R., They Dared the Deep (Pelham, 1968)
Masters, D., When Ships Go Down (Eyre & Spottiswood, 1932)
    S.O.S. (Eyre & Spottiswood, 1937)

Divers in Deep Seas (Eyre & Spottiswood, 1938)
Wonders of Salvage (Eyre & Spottiswood, 1944)
Matkin and Brookes, Snorkel Diver (Macdonald, 1961)
Scuba Diver (Macdonald, 1961)
McCormick, Allen and Young, Shadow in the Sea (Chilton, 1963)
McDonald, K., ed., The Underwater Book (Pelham, 1968)
ed., The Second Underwater Book (Pelham, 1970)
How to Get More Fun from Your Boat (Pelham, 1969)
More Than Skin Deep (Pelham, 1971)
The Wreck Detectives (Harrap, 1972)
ed., The World Underwater Book (Pelham, 1973)
McKee, A., The Golden Wreck (Souvenir, 1961)
History Under the Sea (Hutchinson, 1968)
The Mary Rose (Souvenir, 1973)
Mew, F., Back of the Wight (County Press, 1934)
Miles, S., Underwater Medicine (Staples, 1976)
Morris, R., Island Treasure (1970, 3rd impression)
Murray and Hjort, Depths of the Oceans
Murray, J., The Ocean (Home University Library, 1913)

Needham, J. G., Life of Inland Waters (1916)
Newbolt, H., Submarine and Anti-Submarine (1918)
New Science of Skin and Scuba Diving (Darton, Longman & Todd, 1962)
Newton, Handbook of British Seaweeds (British Museum)
Norman, J. R., History of Fishes (Benn, 1947)

Ommaney, F. D., The Ocean (Oxford University Press, 1949)
Collecting Sea Shells (Arco)
Owen, D. M., Manual for Free Divers (Pergamon, 1955)

Parish, S., Australia's Ocean of Life (Wedneil, 1974)
Peterson, M., History Under the Sea (Smithsonian Institute)
Petron and Lozet, Guinness Guide to Underwater Life (Guinness, 1975)
Petterson, H., The Ocean Floor (1954)
Piccard and Diez, Seven Miles Down (Longmans, 1962)
Piccard, J., The Sun Beneath the Sea (Hale, 1971)
Portman, A., Wonders of the Sea
Poulet and Marincou, Complete Guide to Underwater Swimming (Newnes, 1964)
Prosperi, Lord of the Sharks (Hutchinson, 1955)
Proudman, J., Dynamical Oceanography (1953)

Quilici, F., The Blue Continent (Weidenfeld & Nicholson, 1954)

Raitt, H., Exploring the Deep Pacific (Norton, 1956)

Ratigan, W., Great Lakes Shipwrecks and Survivors (Eerdmans, 1960)

Ray and Ciampi, Underwater Guide to Marine Life (Kaye, 1958)

Rebikoff, D., Free Diving (1955)

Rebikoff and Cherney, Guide to Underwater Photography (Chilton, 1965)

Rieseberg, H., and Mikalow, A., Sunken Treasure Ships of the World (Fell, 1965)

Rogers, S., Derelicts of the Sea (1937)

Roghi and Bascheri, Dahlak (Kaye, 1956)

Schenk and Kendall, Underwater Photography (Cornell Maritime Press, 1954)

    Shallow Water Diving and Spearfishing (Cornell Maritime Press)

Scott, D., Seventy Fathoms Deep (Faber, 1931)

    The Egypt's Gold (Faber, 1932)

Shelford, W. O., Subsunk (Harrap, 1961)

Shroeder, R. E., Something Rich and Strange (Allen & Unwin, 1967)

Skuse, G., Mask, Fins and Snorkel (Swimming Teachers' Association, 1971)

Slack, J., Finders Losers (Hutchinson, 1968)

Small, P., Your Guide to Underwater Adventure (1957)

Steers, J. A., Coastline of England and Wales (Collins, 1966)

Stenuit, R., The Deepest Days (Hodder & Stoughton, 1966)

    Treasures of the Armada (David & Charles, 1972)

Step, Shell Life (Warne)

Tailliez, P., To Hidden Depths (W. Kimber, 1954)

    Aquarius (Harrap, 1964)

Tassos, J., The Underwater World

Tazieff, H., South from the Red Sea (Lutterworth, 1956)

Thompson, C. W., Depths of the Sea (1873)

Throckmorton, P., The Lost Ships (Cape, 1964)

    Shipwrecks and Archaeology (Gollancz)

Titcombe, R., Handbook for Professional Divers (A. Coles, 1973)

Travis Jenkins, J., Fishes of the British Isles (Warne, 1958)

Treanor, T. S., Heroes of the Goodwin Sands (Religious Tract Society, 1892)

Uhl, R., Treasures in the Depths (Oldbourne, 1957)

Underwater Archaeology (Unesco, 1972)

Underwater Treasures (National Geographic Society, 1974)

U.S. Navy Diving Manual (Navy Department, 1970)

Wagener, A., Origin of the Oceans (1924)

Wagner, K., Pieces of Eight (Longmans, 1967)

Waldron and Gleeson, The Frogmen (Evans, 1950)
Walker, S. F., Submarine Engineering (C. Arthur Pearson, 1914)
Warren and Benson, Above Us The Waves (Harrap, 1953)
Webster Smith, B., The World Under the Sea (1939)
Wells, A. L., Observer's Sea Fishes (Warne, 1958)
    Observer's Freshwater Fishes (Warne, 1941)
Wheeler, A., Fishes of the British Isles and North-West Europe (Macmillan)
Whitehouse, A., Sub and Submariners (Muller, 1963)
White and Hadfield, Deep Sea Salvage (Samson Low)
Whittaker, R., One Clear Call (Pelham, 1962)
Williamson, J. E., Twenty Years Under the Sea (Bodley Head, 1935)
Wilson, D. P., Life of the Shore and Shallow Sea (Nicholas & Watson, 1935)
    They Live in the Sea (1947)
Wimpenny, Plankton of the Sea (Faber)
Wright, B. S., The Frogmen of Burma (Kimber)
Wilkes, B. St. John, Nautical Archaeology (David & Charles, 1971)

Young, D., The Man in the Helmet (Cassell, 1963)

Zanelli, L., Teach Yourself Underwater Swimming (English Universities Press, 1967)
    Diving Around Britain (Aquaphone, 1968)
    ed., Underwater Swimming – An Advanced Handbook (Kaye & Ward, 1968)
    Shipwrecks Around Britain (Kaye & Ward, 1970)
    ed., Production of Air For Breathing from Compressors (BSAC, 1970)
    The Sub-Aqua Guide (Sub-Aqua magazine, 1972-76)
    ed., British Sub-Aqua Club Diving Manual (BSAC, editions 1968, 70, 72, 74)
    ed., The Diver's Swimline Search (BSAC, 1972)
    Unknown Shipwrecks Around Britain (Kaye & Ward, 1974)
    Subaqua Swimming (Teach Yourself Books, 1976)